ENGLAND'S CRISIS

ENGLAND'S CRISIS

BY

ANDRÉ SIEGFRIED

TRANSLATED FROM THE FRENCH BY

H. H. HEMMING *&* DORIS HEMMING

HARCOURT, BRACE AND COMPANY

NEW YORK

COPYRIGHT, 1931, BY

HARCOURT, BRACE AND COMPANY, INC.

first edition

PRINTED IN THE UNITED STATES OF AMERICA
BY QUINN & BODEN COMPANY, INC., RAHWAY, N. J.

CONTENTS

6 CONTENTS

CONTENTS

TRANSLATORS' NOTE

WHAT is wrong with England? Are her industries suffering from a chronic malady, or is her unemployment only a passing disorder? What are the real causes of the present severe depression? Is England the victim of circumstances which are beyond her control, or is "the fault, dear Brutus, not in our stars but in ourselves"? Should England try to consolidate her Empire, linking it together with economic as well as sentimental ties, or should she keep a tight grip on the time-honoured principles of Free Trade and internationalism that made her great in the nineteenth century? What attitude should she adopt towards the United States?

These and similar questions are being asked not only in England and throughout the British Empire, but also in foreign countries, for today it is universally recognized that we have reached a crossroads in our history. The interest which is being shown in our problems by the rest of the world is not simply academic, for the fate of no other country, with the possible exception of the United States, is so vital to the future welfare and tranquillity of mankind.

The keenest of foreign observers, consequently, are constrained to analyze and discuss our affairs. It is well for us that they should do so, for although the final decision rests with ourselves, we are bound to benefit from an impartial study written without party prejudice or national bias. We in England are too close to the problem. We cannot see beyond the surface, but the foreign writer looks from a distance straight into the heart of the matter. He penetrates with unerring instinct and diagnoses relentlessly.

Much of this book will prove bitter reading to the thoughtful Englishman, who may be tempted to deny indignantly many of Professor Siegfried's conclusions. Nevertheless, although his observations may be mercilessly logical, he is actuated by genuine affection and admiration for this country.

Professor Siegfried comes of a distinguished Alsatian family, which has long been noted for its political ability. Since he graduated in Paris in 1898 he has devoted his life to the study and teaching of political science, having now been for many years a professor at the Ecole Libre des Sciences Politiques. He has specialized in the economic and political development of the Anglo-Saxon nations, having written books on England, Canada, New Zealand, and three years ago on the United States. As a result of the latter book, *America Comes of Age,* he is today recognized internationally as one of the most brilliant observers and lucid thinkers among modern economists.

His contact with England has been long and intimate. During the past thirty years he has visited us regularly, and has lectured before British audiences on many occasions. He was for several years attached to the British Army during the War. Not long ago he spent some time at Oxford at All Souls, where he studied the situation from close range.

Although his present survey of conditions in England may seem severe and critical, his faith in the courage and virility of the British race is unshaken. He sincerely believes that we shall rally from the stunning blow dealt us by the present crisis, and maintain our place as a leader in international affairs.

We have much pleasure in extending our thanks to Miss Alice Weaver for her assistance and co-operation in the work of this translation.

H. H. HEMMING.
DORIS HEMMING.

LONDON, 1931.

ENGLAND'S CRISIS

INTRODUCTION

BRITAIN IN THE NINETEENTH CENTURY

To TURN the corner from the nineteenth into the twentieth century, there, in a word, is the whole British problem. It is largely because that delicate transition was still unaccomplished by 1914, that England is suffering today from a crisis, the intensities of which can scarcely be exaggerated. Although almost a third of the present century has passed, Great Britain still depends on an economic structure and on methods which often definitely belong to the previous century. She sits on her little island out of contact with the rest of the world, for in this "happy valley" time does not seem to flow as quickly as elsewhere. England still lives in the atmosphere of the past, and this is one of the secrets of her extraordinary charm. But if she wishes to continue as one of the great powers of the world, or, indeed, to exist at all, a complete revision is imperative. Such a theme will be the leitmotiv of this book.

I. FREE TRADE AND BRITAIN'S SUPREMACY

As time goes on it becomes daily more apparent that during the last hundred years England has relied upon conditions which she believed to be permanent, but which are now proving transitory.

Reviewing the British economic system as a whole, we find that its pre-eminence coincided historically with the reign of the steam engine. The Victorian Era, high-water mark of England's prosperity and power, was based on coal, for as long as England's mines enjoyed a quasi-monopoly and coal was the only fuel used by industry, so long her manufactures were practically unrivalled. Also, as her cost prices were the lowest anywhere, she captured the world's markets almost without resistance. She was thus able to create a paradoxical structure of over-developed factories in a restricted and not particularly suitable territory. At the same time a population grew up which today is too congested and too dangerously dependent for its subsistence on imported products.

In nineteenth-century Britain a map of the coal basins represented the industrial skeleton of the nation, but this may not be so in the future. Such a map showed how firmly the industrial structure, the distribution of the population, and the real sources of the nation's energy, were definitely fixed in the grimy manufacturing north. This Black Country was more industrious, more Protestant, and sturdier in spirit than the "Merry Old England" of the south. Coal acted like a magnet, attracting to it the life of the nation. The headquarters of the country's activity did not lie in the London of those days, but was divided between London and Manchester; this is hardly true today.

Under these conditions the doctrine of Free Trade was particularly apt; it seems to have been conceived especially for England by a Providence at once attentive and partial. Liberal doctrines and self-interest concided so exactly that selfishness and disinterested humanitarianism became indistinguishable. Although the English have a stronger sense of nationality than most European peoples, they are also the most dependent on international prosperity. Banking and commerce live on trade, and naturally desire the greatest possible liberty. Industries which produced cheaply and exported extensively—often, indeed, the greater part of their output—thought the same way. What had they to gain from protection? In those days there was complete agreement between the three main branches of economic activity, for it was in the interests of each that British capital should assist in the creation of new customers abroad. Similarly, it was to the advantage of banking and commerce that a prosperous industry should maintain a steady volume of transactions, for without this movement of real merchandise financial activities would lack a genuine foundation. A pre-established harmony existed, since none of the partners could be accused of making use of the others without assisting them in return.

It was a sign of decadence, therefore, when immediately after the War the City imposed a monetary policy which strangled industry, and the latter, in self-defence, evolved a system of protection which threatened commerce and finance. The very fact that a choice had to be made, and that any choice, whatever it was, was bound to hurt some one, showed that the system was seriously out of order.

The Victorians were conscious of their superiority, as they lived in the stimulating atmosphere of rapidly accumulating wealth. They profited by that mysterious extra speed which seems to spur on those who start first, for they were the first fully to exploit the Industrial Revolution which transformed the world, and gave to Europe uncontested economic control. The atmosphere of America today can be used as an analogy to give some idea of the animation that must have pervaded England in the nineteenth century.

Such magnificent success naturally produced a feeling of immense and well-founded pride. To realize England's grandeur, her rulers, her thinkers, and even her tourists, had only to look around them. They congratulated themselves on their possession of the basis of power in a world reborn through the steam engine.

"The length of our coast-line, which is greater in proportion to our population and territory than in the case of any other nation, assures our strength and maritime superiority. Iron and coal—the nerves of industry—give our manufacturers great advantages over our rivals, and our capital exceeds what they can dispose of. In invention, in energy, in ability, we yield to no one. Our national character, the free institutions under which we live, our liberty of thought and action, our untrammelled press which spreads abroad our discoveries and progress—all these things place us in the forefront of the nations

which develop mutually by the free exchange of
their products. Is this a country which should fear
competition?" In his great speech in the House of
Commons in 1846, on the Abolition of the Corn
Laws, Sir Robert Peel made the above simple statement of incontestable facts. The pre-eminence of
coal and iron carried everything before it. Michelet
has summed up the situation in his vivid description of England as *un bloc de fer et de houille.*

Twenty years later, when free trade had already
borne fruit, the situation was even more favourable,
and the daring of Cobden and his school was entirely justified. In 1860 Stanley Jevons, whose capacity for pessimism we shall presently discover,
wrote as follows: "Unfettered commerce, founded
on the basis of our coal resources, has made the
several quarters of the globe our willing tributaries.
The plains of North America and Russia are our
corn fields; Chicago and Odessa our granaries;
Canada and the Baltic our forests; Australasia contains our sheep farms, and in South America are our
herds of oxen. Peru sends her silver, and the gold of
California and Australia flows to London; the Chinese grow tea for us, and coffee, sugar and spice arrive from the East Indian plantations. Spain and

France are our vineyards, and the Mediterranean our fruit garden; our cotton grounds, which formerly occupied the Southern United States, are now everywhere in the many regions of the earth. . . ."

At about the same time Sir Charles Dilke, who on leaving the university made a voyage around the world, completed his surveys on a triumphant political note: "In 1866 and 1867 I followed England round the world; everywhere I was in English-speaking or in English-governed lands. . . . The idea which in all my travels has been at once my fellow and my guide is a conception, however imperfect, of the grandeur of our race."

This was the opinion of the English nation, and Europe, though jealous, shared it. It found expression in the works of Jules Verne, who began to write at that time. On every page of *Round the World in Eighty Days,* or *The Secret of the Island,* one feels his admiration for the English, whom he considered men of energy and inflexible determination, magnificent egotists, always in the van of technical progress and humanitarian activities. Twenty of his other novels are devoted to the same epic theme: the conquest of the planet by modern science aided by character. Prior to 1870 the French loved to call

themselves *La Grande Nation,* but the expression
was more applicable to England in her great period
of free trade.

2. LIMITS OF BRITAIN'S SUPREMACY

The initiators of the new economic *régime,*
Richard Cobden and Sir Robert Peel, clearly realized the sacrifices that would accompany the whole-
hearted adoption of free trade. The eventual decline
of agriculture had to be faced, for a policy of low
prices necessitates unrestricted imports, which are
apt to be contrary to the best interests of the farm-
ing community. The nation, therefore, had to learn
to live on imported food, and the factories to use
foreign raw materials in steadily growing quanti-
ties. These purchases abroad were to be paid for
by exports. Since both soil and climate are mediocre
in Great Britain, industrialism had to be pushed
relentlessly to its utmost limits. There could be no
possible hope of economic independence, for not
merely had Britain to accept a division of labour
which led to specialization, but also the risks which
accompany international interdependence. Still, the
advantages could be amazing.

For a whole century England has tried out the

experiment. In spite of its perfections there are many grave risks attendant on this system, for it is based on certain hypotheses which are not necessarily permanent. England's success was due to the coincidence of a variety of exceptional circumstances.

International division of labour had to be accepted without question, making England, and to a lesser extent Western Europe, the highly specialized workshop of the world. The entire doctrine was based on this principle, which had been inherited from the days of the Colonial Pact. The colonies were to produce the raw materials which the mother country reserved the right to transform into manufactured goods, and it was assumed that the non-European countries would maintain towards Europe the deferential attitude of a colony towards the motherland. Otherwise there would have been no sense in the concentration on a few square miles in the British Isles of an over-developed industry, and the accumulation there of a dense population which in the last resource must depend for its existence less on the products of the soil than on the margin of profit realized by the exporting industries. There was no guarantee that the new countries would not one day wish to manufacture their own raw materials nor that England's cost of production would always be lower than that of her competitors. This last consideration is really the key to the whole problem.

Still another hypothesis is inevitable, namely that there should be absolute free trade, not only internationally, but within the country itself. Tariff freedom should be accompanied by liberty in labour and wages, which should react spontaneously to any change in prices. It was not without reason that Cobden and his epoch viewed with suspicion the social aspects of the labour problem. The Liberal school considered labour as merchandise, and refused to speak of it except in economic terms. About 1840, when they extolled the free entry of foreign wheat, they argued that if bread were cheaper, wages would be lowered, and thus without affecting the standard of living of the workmen, manufacturing costs could be considerably relieved. If wages had been blocked by social legislation, the reaction on which they counted would not have taken place, and the system would not have worked.

Finally it was essential that coal should enjoy the monopoly bestowed upon it by the steam engine, and that England should maintain her extraordinary lead in this field. In 1868-70, out of the world's coal production of 130 million tons, England accounted for 80 millions. But would Prussia always turn out only 12 million tons, and the United States only 14 millions?

These hypotheses were readily admitted by contemporary thinkers, but today we realize the imprudence of accepting as normal a mere stage in the economic evolution of the world, and of constructing on this foundation an edifice which it is now difficult to modify. The situation may have been sound at the time it was consolidated, but it was none the less precarious, for the margin of supply was too small. According to Nietzsche's phrase, England agreed "to live dangerously." As a matter of fact, this remark also applied to Europe in this period of its expansion, but to a lesser degree, for in the great game of consequences it was England that became most involved.

Towards 1866, Stanley Jevons, with his penetrating mind, perceived the essential fragility of the system, which is the theme of his prophetic book, *The Coal Question*. England, he contended, owed her pre-eminence less to merit than to her mining monopoly, and he laid stress on the fact that coal is capital which is being used up, and not a crop which can be resown annually. Should the coal seams become exhausted, or should coal be obtainable only at a steadily increasing cost, then manufacturing would become uneconomic and exporting correspondingly difficult. The situation would be relatively the same if British coal were to lose its monopoly, for were coal to be mined elsewhere, new industrial centres would arise in other parts of the world. This would bring the menace of unemployment to an England over-equipped and over-populated. The only courses of action open to her would be mass emigration or a permanent lowering of the standard of living.

The coal supply, however, has not become exhausted as was feared, but it no longer enjoys its unique position, for oil and hydro-electric power are wresting from it a growing share of its former domain. As England has little hydro-electric power, and is forced to import all her oil, she is no longer the most favoured nation. Even from the standpoint of coal itself her days of supremacy are over, for the United States has long since outstripped her, and

Germany, Poland, and even France are serious rivals. Therefore, the doubts of Stanley Jevons, that English Cassandra of 1866, have tended to materialize in the twentieth century, for all the complications which he foretold have come to pass, though in a slightly different form. His book is prophetic, and can be read today as a merciless analysis of the present difficulties of Great Britain.

3. FIRST SIGNS OF DECLINE

If we begin our study of England at the economic high-water mark of 1860-70, we can soon trace the first symptoms of decline, for the sources of the present crisis are to be found as far back as 1880. It was then that the first serious rivals began to appear, for hitherto British industry had stood alone. The report, published in 1886, by the Royal Commission appointed to enquire into the Depression of Trade and Industry, leaves no doubt on this score. Conditions were already disquieting, and England should have made an effort to recover or at least to adapt herself to the changes that were then taking place. Instead we find her calmly resting on her laurels. She enjoyed a complete monopoly not only in distant countries, but even in Europe, where individualism was still backward, and without realizing it, she was accustomed to all that this monopoly entailed. She honestly believed that she was competing internationally under normal conditions, without guile and according to the rules of Free Trade. In reality, however, her commercial victories were less important than she thought, because she had not encountered a dangerous rival until she met the Germany of William II. Insular temperamentally as well as geographically, she is apt to consider all foreigners—even Europeans—as second-raters, living on a plane inferior to her own. The legendary Englishman who remarked that "the negroes begin at Calais," was only joking no doubt, but in his heart of hearts he meant what he said.

As a result of this regal security the qualities of ferocious energy and dogged striving with gritted teeth, which the rest of the world has been pleased to attribute to the Englishman, are the very ones which in business seem to have died out. The inherited habits of wealth and power have bestowed on him an aristocratic manner, curiously mixed with a belief in the divine right of his race. Now that British supremacy is questioned, this attitude is even more accentuated. At the close of the century, a new generation was born with ideas of abundance and glory. They became accustomed to a comfortable life in which money came easily, and unconsciously they persuaded themselves that success was their due.

It was about ten or fifteen years after the War of 1870, at a time when German economic rivalry was just beginning to be felt, that the English drifted into the way of arriving late at work and leaving early. The week-ends were surreptitiously extended —Saturday mornings and even Monday mornings were lost. In the Far East, where England's position was soon to be attacked, English stores were the last to open, and somehow seemed to shut again almost immediately. In the same concessions the Germans were working ten hours a day, and the Chinese fourteen. Prodigality became a distinct trait in the British character, not to mention a subtle trace of laziness. True, English economic technique was still marvellous, for it was based on years of experience. During working hours their output is excellent, and time is not wasted as in France, yet they become steadily more unwilling to sacrifice their leisure to business.

Owing to these defects—which many do not consider to be defects—nineteenth-century England evolved a conception of life that is original and charming, permeated by modern ideas of comfort and leisure, and a thoroughly civilized appreciation of the pleasures of life. Contrary to appearances, this civilization unfits a man for the struggle for existence. "Why strain myself in crude economic pursuits," says the gentleman, "when overwork uses up my strength and saps my vitality?" So he looks for results without effort, and gradually comes to consider as unfair the competition of those who deny themselves in order to succeed, and work longer hours than he does.

If at this point in her destiny England had been forced by some accident to reform, who knows what might have happened? Suppose that instead of a few colonial expeditions she had been engaged in a really serious war, or suppose that the long-drawn-out Victorian Era had come prematurely to an end! The Old Queen was the symbol of the eternal, changeless stability of things, of the abundance in which the English had lived for generations, and the easy profits they still earned with no serious effort to reorganize. The whole structure of the kingdom seemed justified. It was an acquired situation, consolidated by Providence, and destined to endure for ever.

Meanwhile, contemporary thinkers, with characteristic British honesty, observed and commented on the first disquieting symptoms of decline. The report of the Commission of Enquiry into the Economic Depression (1886) is a monument of lucid objectivity, and a dozen similar reports have followed it. "What courage!" we exclaim. "What realists! How calmly they look straight into the bottom of the abyss!" For over forty years the Blue Books have been perpetually repeating the same grave warnings. "We are no longer alone. More active rivals with better equipment are springing up and leaving us behind. . . ." So ran the Enquiry in 1886, and in 1930 in his report on British Commerce in South America Lord d'Abernon uses the same terms, makes the same reproaches, and reveals the same defects in the Britain of today.

In France we could never be so objective; but why is all this heart-searching so sterile? Simply this: intellectually the Englishman reads and appreciates these warnings, but by instinct he refuses to believe them. His unshaken confidence in his country, his pride, and an extraordinary faculty of not seeing what he prefers to ignore, all rebel against the lesson. He juggles with it, and finally drops it altogether. A sanctimonious and inherent optimism whispers that he will pull through somehow, not because he has seen how his methods can be reformed, or his equipment renewed, but simply because he is an Englishman. "We will muddle through," he says. But if this formula is to work out in practice it will be because England is borne along on the incoming tide.

4. BRITAIN IN THE TWENTIETH CENTURY

Obviously Old England has been living in a fool's paradise, fondly imagining that she could still rely on the spirit and methods of the nineteenth century. Such reforms as have been attempted are insignificant; at any rate, up to the War no serious efforts were made to transform coal mining, the metal industry, or textiles—the three bases on which exports and prosperity were founded. England is like a venerable mansion, which though well and solidly built, has for years lacked repairs both inside and out.

The blow which struck the country in 1921 revealed a dangerous breach in her economic fortifications. In the tumult of the War and the post-War period, public opinion was misled as to the nature and extent of the trouble, which was considered only a passing storm arising out of the world conflict and likely to die down as soon as stability was regained. The English especially counted on the return of pre-War conditions, but little by little their hopes were dissipated, and since the General Strike of 1926 they have been wondering whether the good old days will ever come back. Seen from this angle the crisis changes in character, as its causes appear to go deeper and be more remote than the War itself. The world has been completely transformed, and in it the England of yesterday has not yet found itself. This recalls the fears of Stanley Jevons, and the first attacks upon the British monopoly as far back as 1880. So long a period of incubation intensifies the gravity of the situation, and points to a chronic lack of adjustment far surpassing the temporary trouble of the War.

The British people as a whole have not yet realized the gravity of the situation, and as their optimism is a mixture of patriotism and lethargy, it can hardly be undermined. Nevertheless, their best brains no longer ignore the fact that a heavy burden of reorganization must be faced. Some still think that a few changes in the Cabinet or the personnel of the Government would be sufficient, but the task is far more difficult than that. Every Englishman must modify his way of working, of thinking, and even of living—in fact, this is just as essential as a change in the foundations on which the country is based.

The acknowledgment on the part of the governing classes that revision is necessary, and that the past is dead, marks the end for England of the post-War period. It also confirms the fact that with the present decade passes the era of unrivalled British supremacy, marked in history by two great milestones, 1815 and 1914.

PART I

THE POST-WAR CRISIS

CHAPTER I

CAUSES AND EXTENT OF THE CRISIS

I. SHRINKAGE OF EXPORTS

IT WAS at the close of the year 1920, after the collapse of the feverish post-War boom, that England was stricken down. After a hundred years of prosperity, adversity came as suddenly as a Biblical plague, and humbled her in her pride. One recalls the opening words of the Book of Job:

"There was a man in the land of Uz, whose name was Job; and that man was perfect and upright, and one that feared God, and eschewed evil.

"And there were born unto him seven sons and three daughters.

"His substance also was seven thousand sheep, and three thousand camels, and five hundred yoke of oxen, and five hundred she-asses, and a very great household; so that this man was the greatest of all the men of the East. . . .

"And there was a day when his sons and his

daughters were eating and drinking wine in their eldest brother's house:

"And there came a messenger unto Job, and said, The oxen were ploughing, and the asses feeding beside them:

"And the Sabeans fell upon them, and took them away; yea, they have slain the servants with the edge of the sword; and I only am escaped alone to tell thee.

"While he was yet speaking, there came also another, and said, The fire of God has fallen from Heaven, and hath burned up the sheep and the servants, and consumed them; and I only am escaped alone to tell thee.

"While he was yet speaking there came also another, and said, The Chaldeans made out three bands, and fell upon the camels, and have carried them away, yea, and slain the servants with the edge of the sword; and I only am escaped alone to tell thee.

"While he was yet speaking there came also another, and said, Thy sons and thy daughters were eating and drinking wine in their eldest brother's house:

"And, behold, there came a great wind from the

wilderness, and smote the four corners of the house, and it fell upon the young men, and they are dead; and I only am escaped alone to tell thee."

Let us translate this story into terms applicable to modern forms of wealth. Every year since 1921 statistics, those merciless modern messengers, have been warning England that she is losing her markets, and that her industrial structure is trembling on its foundations. As in the Book of Job, "There came a great wind from the wilderness, and smote the four corners of the house."

The crisis can be most easily gauged by the serious fall in exports. The figures take their full significance when they are amended in conformity with the 1913 price level.

BRITISH EXPORTS

	Millions of Pounds Sterling	Percentage Reduced to 1914 Price Level
1913	525	100
1920	1,334	71
1921	703	50
1927	709	79
1929	730	82

If this shrinkage of one-fifth persists, and if in the future England's share of the world trade is to

be no greater than at present, then the national
economic structure must be completely reorganized
on a new foundation. Otherwise the overloaded ship
is in danger of running aground, for the waters are
too shallow.

Comparison with other countries is not reassuring. From 1913 to 1927 British exports declined 21
per cent., but during the same period we find that the
world's export trade instead of falling rose 18 per
cent., and further, in the case of the Dominions and
the United States, the increases were 31 per cent.
and 51 per cent. respectively.

England, however, is not the only sufferer, for
European trade also has declined. The British share
of world exports decreased from 13.9 per cent. to
11.2 per cent. between 1913 and 1928, while the
European exports fell from 55.2 per cent. to 46
per cent. This classes Great Britain with the older
countries of Western Europe, instead of with the
newer communities of her empire, as she would
prefer.

These figures are serious, and particularly so
when applied to an exporting country. The great
British industries, on which the economic structure
of the country is still based, used to export at least

two-fifths of their total production, and in some cases even three-quarters.

For example, the following are the approximate proportions exported during the post-War period:

Cottons	75%
Woollens	45% to 48%
Linen	50%
Jute	40%
Iron and Steel	40% to 50%

Though coal exports are low in comparison with the total mined, being about 25 per cent., they are exceedingly important because they provide outgoing cargoes. This is a delicate point in the British structure, and one which must be protected at all cost. Since the War the exports of each of these basic industries, without exception, have suffered serious injury. Cotton, most important of all, has had the total volume of its foreign sales reduced by over one-third, and worse still, this decrease appears to be permanent. If this is so it means that certain essential parts of the economic machine have been impaired. Lord Derby was absolutely right when he referred to foreign trade as "the devastated areas of British industry."

With their characteristic optimism, even in the face of despair, the English long hoped against hope.

Each month the unfavourable statistics were interpreted as heralds of better days. But the better days
did not arrive, and in 1930 a second world crisis
overcame the British economic system before it had
recovered from the crisis of 1921. The permanent
nature of the depression has now at last alarmed the
thoughtful.

2. UNEMPLOYMENT

If the chief indication of the economic crisis is
the falling off in exports, the most apparent social
consequence is the agonizing amount of unemployment. The immediate cause of this state of affairs is
the lack of a sufficient margin of profit for the manufacturer. In a country supporting a maximum population on the hypothesis that profitable exports can
always be relied upon, any depression in foreign
trade naturally produces grave disturbances. If the
slump lasts until there is little hope of speedy recovery, then it becomes a catastrophe.

The phenomenon of unemployment has constantly
recurred in England at regular intervals. In 1879
it amounted to 11 per cent. of the total industrial
workers, and in 1886 to 10 per cent.; since 1874 it
has never been less than 2 per cent. Throughout the

nineteenth century and until the Great War, however, the depressions never lasted any length of time in an acute form, as they were only symptoms of congestion. The gravest feature of the present phase, which began in 1920-21, and of which the end is not yet in sight, is its permanency rather than its intensity.

UNEMPLOYMENT

		Total Number Unemployed	Percentage of Insured Workers
1921	January	1,010,000	6.4
	July	2,508,000	15.5
1922	January	2,003,000	14.2
	July	1,423,000	12.6
1923	January	1,511,000	13.3
	July	1,226,000	11.6
1924	January	1,268,000	11.9
	July	1,025,000	9.8
1925	January	1,307,000	11.2
	July	1,300,000	11.2
1926	January	1,252,000	11.1
	July	1,645,000	14.6
1927	January	1,496,000	12.1
	July	1,054,000	9.3
1928	January	1,336,000	10.7
	July	1,217,000	11.6
1929	January	1,453,000	12.1
	July	1,142,000	9.7
1930	January	1,479,000	12.6
	July	2,070,000	17.1

Allowing for seasonable variations which swell unemployment in the autumn and diminish it in the spring, we find that the above table gives a faithful outline of British economic history during recent years. Unemployment can be compared to a flood: the waters rise when world tempests are raging (1920-21, 1930-31), and every country, without exception, is inundated until they subside. In England, however, the situation is different, for apparently there is a certain level below which the flood never ebbs. A million unemployed seems to be the minimum. The figures dropped below that point only in April 1926 and May and June 1927, and then merely by a few thousands. We must not be too impressed by the two million unemployed in 1930; the real problem is the permanent million.

These percentages indicate only the average of the country as a whole, so in order to determine the root of the evil we must ascertain which branches of industry are most affected. With this in view let us examine the extent of unemployment, industry by industry, at five representative dates of which three, 1921, 1926, and 1930, are bad periods, while two, 1923 and 1928, are at moments of comparative recovery.

PERCENTAGE OF UNEMPLOYED COMPARED WITH THE

TOTAL MAN-POWER IN DIFFERENT

INDUSTRIES

(July Figures)

	1921 [1]	1923	1926	1928	1930
Coal	8.1	3.0	8.8	29.1	28.3
Shipbuilding	32.8	43.2	41.5	28.3	31.7
Engineering	23.0	20.9	17.5	9.7	16.7
Iron and Steel	48.8	19.9	66.2	21.2	28.5
Cottons	10.5	21.3	28.1	15.2	44.7
Woollens	14.6	9.3	23.3	15.1	26.1
Commerce	6.7	5.9	6.6	5.2	8.3
Building Trades ...	14.9	12.2	9.4	10.4	13.9

[1] The 1921 figures are not exactly comparable with those of other years, because of a slightly different classification existing at that time.

It is immediately apparent that the storm centre is not in the same position throughout the whole of this period. In 1921 iron and steel, engineering, and shipbuilding, were the principal industries to suffer, but from 1926 onwards it was coal and then cottons. In the latter industry the situation became absolutely tragic by 1930. Whatever may account for these variations, one central fact emerges, *i.e.* that the sufferers at both the beginning and the end of the decade were all exporting industries, and, moreover, the very ones which in the nineteenth century were the keystone of Britain's prosperity.

It may be argued that these same industries suffered
during the post-War depression in other countries
also, but there they were neither so exclusively exporting nor so essential to the national welfare. In
the England of Cobden, Peel, and Gladstone, coal,
iron, and steel, and the textile trades, could be
counted on to absorb the surplus population, but
today they are unable to do so, and are on the contrary flooding the labour market with their unemployed. As these basic industries no longer function
properly, the State is becoming congested by the excess of population. This observation is confirmed
and developed by a study of the geographic distribution of unemployment. Let us take the month
of May 1928, for at that time the depression from
which the country suffered was specifically British,
and not world-wide as in 1930. (See maps, pages
46-47.)

Three zones stand out clearly, according to our
maps. The first in the north covers the entire Black
Country where industry is based on coal. Everywhere we find unemployment amounting to over
10 per cent. (the average for the whole country was
9.8 per cent.), and the proportion even exceeds 15
per cent. in two coal mining districts, Northumber-

land-Durham and South Wales (Durham, 23 per cent.; Glamorgan, 24 per cent.).

The second zone lies on the south-east border of the first, and includes a region of secondary manufacturing where the heavy industries do not dominate. This area is undoubtedly less affected. In the counties of Gloucester, Warwick, Northampton, and Nottingham it varies from 5 to 10 per cent., and in Leicester it is less than 5 per cent.

In the third area we have London, the home counties grouped around London principally in the valley of the Thames, and in general the entire south of England. This district has scarcely suffered at all, for there is only 4.4 per cent. of unemployment in London, 3.9 per cent. in Middlesex, 3.8 per cent. in Bedfordshire, 3.5 per cent. in Oxfordshire, 2.8 per cent. in Surrey and 2.6 per cent. in Sussex. If we turn to our map of unemployment, which shows the actual numbers unemployed instead of the percentage figures, we see how remarkably localized is the evil. (See map, page 47.)

The depression of 1930, although it increased unemployment everywhere, did not change the relationship between these zones. In the first zone there was uniformly more than 15 per cent., in the

UNEMPLOYMENT BY COUNTIES (MAY, 1928)

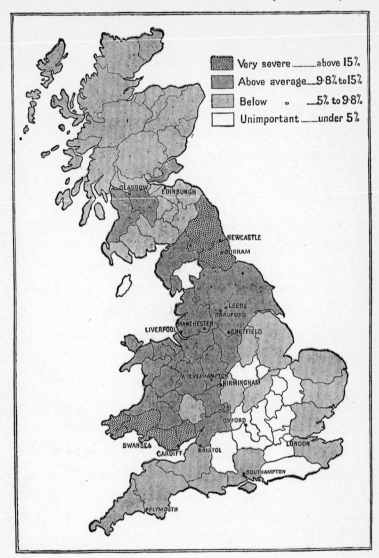

Very severe _____ above 15%
Above average __ 9·8% to 15%
Below   „   __ 5% to 9·8%
Unimportant ____ under 5%

PERCENTAGE OF TOTAL INSURED POPULATION

UNEMPLOYMENT BY COUNTIES (MAY, 1928)

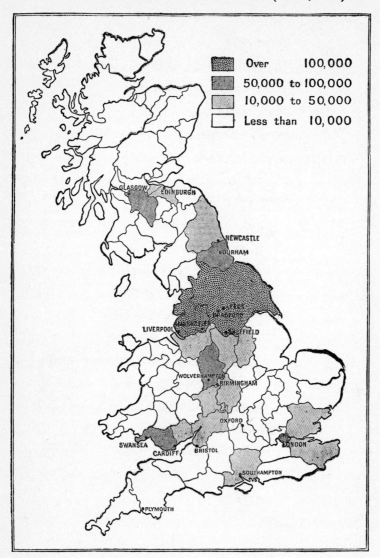

Over   100,000

50,000 to 100,000

10,000 to 50,000

Less than 10,000

GLASGOW

EDINBURGH

NEWCASTLE

DURHAM

BRADFORD

LIVERPOOL

SHEFFIELD

MANCHESTER

WOLVERHAMPTON

BIRMINGHAM

OXFORD

SWANSEA

CARDIFF

BRISTOL

LONDON

SOUTHAMPTON

PLYMOUTH

TOTAL NUMBERS OF UNEMPLOYED

second more than 10 per cent., and in the third more
than 5 per cent. Although there are certain exceptions, the distinction between the three zones still
exists. What is especially noticeable is that unemployment is localized to a marked degree, even within each county. In August 1930, for example, when
the figures passed the two million mark, nearly one-
half of the unemployed were located in the four
counties of Lancashire, Yorkshire, Staffordshire,
and Durham; over three-fifths were in these counties together with Lanarkshire and Glamorgan—
in other words, coal, iron and steel, cotton, and
wool.

This geographical concentration is still more accentuated in the interior of each county. The central towns or regional distribution centres, where
labour is distributed among various branches of
commerce and production, are not particularly hard
hit. In the case of Lancashire only 15.3 per cent.
are unemployed in its capital city, Manchester. It is
the specialized industrial towns of this great cotton
area that have borne the full force of the gale.
Blackburn, with an insured population of 56,000,
has 52.7 per cent. unemployed; Acrington, with
31,000, has 44.3 per cent.; Burnley, with 47,000, has

42.1 per cent.; while many of the smaller towns have even higher percentages.

A similar situation, only worse, exists in the mining districts, where the slowing down or definite closing of a pit will at one fell swoop render idle practically the entire population. The unemployment figures for the county as a whole, however, give an insufficient indication of the total stoppage that sometimes occurs: Glamorgan has 31 per cent. unemployed; Monmouth, 32.7 per cent.; Durham, 26.8 per cent.; Northumberland, 21.5 per cent.; Lanark, 22.6 per cent.; but in certain stricken mining villages the figure is over one-half or even as high as two-thirds, and can theoretically become almost 100 per cent. These are the black spots where all hope has slowly died.

Meanwhile, in the south, the depression remains relatively slight. In August 1930, London had only 6.6 per cent. unemployed; Greater London, 7.1 per cent.; Surrey, 4.6 per cent.; Sussex, 4.2 per cent.; Middlesex, 7.4 per cent.; and Kent, 7.9 per cent.

The map of unemployment is thus approximately the same as the map of the coal areas. What used to be and still is the centre of England's population and industries, is stricken down. Ever since the time

of Cobden these areas have been the focus of the
moral energy of the country. We must not lose sight
of this fact, either in our diagnosis of the ills, or in
our appraisal of eventual recovery.

England finds that she is burdened with a surplus
of about a million workers, whom she cannot profitably employ, although this does not mean that the
same million individuals are totally and permanently
idle. In certain cases, as in the abandoned mining
areas of the north, such a condition may exist, but
taking the country as a whole there is a continual
interchange going on between the workers and the
unemployed. It was found as the result of an interesting enquiry made by the Ministry of Labour,[1]
that between October 1923 and April 1927, out of
8024 men who had been unemployed, 48 per cent.
had received the dole for less than one-fifth of the
time, 26 per cent. for more than one-fifth but less
than half, and 16 per cent. for more than half; only
10 per cent. were unemployed for more than three-
fifths of the time, and it is this 10 per cent. which
constitutes the irreducible minimum of unemployment.

[1] Ministry of Labour Enquiry into 9748 individual cases of unemployment in April 1927.

The same enquiry also revealed that all ages do not suffer alike. As might be expected, among those over forty-five unemployment was greater, and for those over sixty it was well above the average. More surprising, however, was the fact that men from twenty-five to twenty-nine years of age at the time of the enquiry in 1927 constituted a group for whom unemployment was especially serious. These are the youths who were badly brought up during the War, who have never learned a trade, and who never will learn to work.

In spite of the more or less fluid character of unemployment, certain industries have a permanent surplus which they seem manifestly incapable of absorbing. In their report published in 1928 the Industrial Transference Board openly admits this fact: "We do not see how the heavy industries can give a living to all those at present attached to them, or to all those who would normally look to them for a livelihood during the next few years." They estimate the irreducible surplus of the coal industry at 200,000 men. Iron and steel and textiles, it is true, show smaller figures, but they are bad enough, and rationalization, if seriously undertaken, is bound to increase their number.

I do not propose at this point to discuss whether by reducing her standards of comfort and leisure England could increase the "employability" of this part of her population, which is really living at the expense of the rest. Let us simply state that given the living conditions which England inherited from the prosperous nineteenth century, the national system is no longer functioning efficiently, but is exhibiting all the characteristics of a worn-out machine.

3. UNDERLYING CAUSES OF THE CRISIS

Possibly it is inaccurate to apply the word "crisis" in its literal sense to England, for she is suffering from a chronic malady, which has various subordinate aspects and phases. One can, for example, isolate the crisis of 1921 as being a reaction to the War and the still-born boom of 1919. Again, following a partial recovery after the Ruhr occupation, there was the coal dispute in 1925, and the General Strike in 1926 with its lasting effects. Finally, after another recovery, especially in southern England between 1927 and 1929, came the world-wide depression of 1930, which has dealt the country a sledge-hammer blow. In fact, since 1919 England has never been able to regain, even temporarily, her pre-War robustness.

At each successive relapse another organ becomes affected before the previous ills have been cured. Public opinion keeps discovering new causes for the depression, on which the Government, the economists and the Press focus all attention. Each time there has been what might be called a semi-official viewpoint of the situation. A foreigner like myself, who has visited England on various occasions since the War, is impressed both by the seriousness of the economic discussions and by their objectivity. Dare I say that he is intimidated? Later, when he turns the matter over in his mind, he fancies he detects a political bias, or ulterior motive in the scientific arguments advanced.

Immediately after the declaration of peace, by a sort of optical illusion, all the trouble was blamed on the War. No nation was more anxious than Britain to wipe out every trace of the conflict. Confronted with Europe, politically and economically Balkanized, stunned by the sensational collapse of three empires, England felt that she could quite easily recapture her old dominating position, as well as her prosperity, provided Germany and Russia were quickly restored, and also provided the new economic barriers were suppressed, or at any rate lowered. The main thing was to bring back normal conditions of international trade. She considered that her equipment was sufficiently up to date, since it had not been injured by shell-fire. To her the problem appeared to be primarily one of international relations. Next, when inflation swept over the Continent, putting the British markets at the mercy of a host of countries with depreciated currencies, she decided that the monetary disturbance was simply another aspect of the same disorder. Therefore she recommended the stabilization of the currency under the aegis of the pound sterling.

Then came the invasion of the Ruhr, and British public opinion unanimously and noisily declared that if the affairs of the world, and especially of England, did not prosper, France was to blame. Military occupation, clumsily and even maliciously thrown like a monkey-wrench into the delicate economic machine of Germany, was sufficient explanation for the continued unrest in Europe. Finally, after the stabilization of the franc, when gold started to flow steadily towards Paris, deserting the City, it was once again the fault of France that world prices were dropping, to the detriment of British trade. France was not playing the game; she was sterilizing the gold which she was accumulating; she was again impeding the international recovery so urgently desired.

This view is interesting, for it sheds considerable light on the psychology of the British in dealing with these rather delicate matters. One cannot help remarking that England usually looks abroad first for the causes of her difficulties—always they are the fault of some one else. If only this culprit or that would reform, then England might be able to regain her prosperity. It is magnificent, the way she can preach a sermon to the rest of the world, expose their weaknesses, and point out their duties. She arouses the indignation of the countries who know how to behave, against the scallywags whose egotism blinds them to their international duties. A cynical Frenchman enjoys pointing out that when England says, "You must think of others," she really means, "You must think of me." Machiavellism? Not at all, simply rather naïve. Her instinct is to try to restore the conditions which suited her, instead of revising her own standards and adapting them to a world in which they are now out of place.

French opinion is dumbfounded by such arguments, yet they are met even in the most responsible circles. If one suggests that English wages are too high for competition—very well, let the Continental nations raise theirs; that the English working day is too short—reduce your own; that the English standard of living is pretentious—renounce your measly economy, civilize yourselves, be like us, learn how to live! England wishes the mountain to come to Mahomet.

These excuses are not without foundation, of course, but viewed from abroad, especially over a ten-year period, the causes of British depression seem to be clearly divisible into two categories: first, those due to external factors and beyond Britain's control; and second, those originating within the country itself and capable of eventual correction by her own efforts. Each class can also be subdivided into temporary and permanent factors.

First let us consider the external causes. We have the world-wide impoverishment and confusion caused by the Great War, with its aftermath of turmoil, revolution, and civil wars. There is no longer any adjustment between consumption and production, for distribution is not normal. Capital does not flow easily—here it is totally lacking, there it is uselessly accumulating. In short, the economic exploitation of the globe is disorganized, with the result that there is a reduction of purchasing power in various international markets. England as a great exporting nation is naturally the first to suffer; in fact, it is her foreign trade that has borne the full shock of the War. No country has felt the War more directly or more brutally, even admitting that English territory was not violated and that none of her factories were destroyed.

Such causes, however, are temporary, and cannot continue to account for Britain's anaemia. By unduly stressing these factors immediately after the War, the English gave themselves a dangerous excuse for their failure to replace the out-of-date sections of their economic system. No doubt it is better to sail with the tide, but one should not altogether rely upon it.

The trouble lies deeper, and in order to discover the real source we evidently must go back earlier than 1914, perhaps as I have already said, even back to 1875 or 1880. What has really changed to the detriment of England is the economic interrelationship of the continents of the world. Since the beginning of the present century, and even earlier, there has been a tendency for distant countries to contest the industrial monopoly of Western Europe, of which England was the leader. Each country now hopes to convert its own raw materials and export them in manufactured form. Although the War did not originate this movement towards widespread industrialism, it undoubtedly accelerated the pace. At the same time, in spite of the Liberal school, which considers it madness, the doctrine that every State should be economically self-supporting is now generally adopted. This is a definite form of contemporary nationalism, which tends to lay stress on old-fashioned protectionist ideas, so dangerous to British exports. We used to be content with protective duties, which allowed local industries to fight on equal terms with foreign competitors for the home market. Customs duties were then considered a weapon of protection rather than prohibition. Now, however, our neo-protectionism has new aims and new methods, beginning with the principle that the home market should be reserved exclusively for national industries. These are given so great a priority that their profits, thus assured, serve as an export bonus, and permit systematic international dumping.

The widespread decentralization of industry has produced new conditions throughout the world, depriving England of her century-old position. The reduction in the export trade, arising from these causes, must be accepted as permanent.

The purely British causes of the economic depression are complex, but they can be summed up in a single sentence: English manufacturing costs are among the highest in the world. If this situation continues, any economic structure based on exports is faced with inevitable ruin. Can England do anything, or is this evil, by its very nature, one that cannot be grappled with? This is the germ of the British problem.

CHAPTER II

HIGH INDUSTRIAL COSTS

I. THE MONETARY POLICY

IT IS generally admitted today that British industry suffered from the monetary policy adopted in 1918-19, which aimed at bringing the pound sterling back to parity with the dollar. This policy of credit and prestige was the work of the City financiers. The Government adopted it and imposed it upon the industrialists, who were scarcely consulted, and who at first did not realize the severe consequences that it would entail.

The financiers were influenced by the century-old tradition of credit—we pay what we owe—and their determination to maintain London as the world's financial centre. Pride could not permit the pound to be outstripped by that new-comer, the dollar. Owing to its instinctive desire to restore normal conditions, the Government listened to these counsellors, and accepted the task of repaying in their entirety the internal and external obligations of the country. By a formidable Budget effort, the object was achieved by 1925, though the battle was really won during 1923. It was about this time that the eventual economic repercussions were first suspected, although they were not completely evident until after 1925, when it was indeed far too late to retreat.

Experience has now proved that this policy was sacrificing production to commerce. The stability and prestige of the pound sterling were guaranteed, and this assisted the financiers, and also the merchants who operate on margins in the international market. In order that industry should profit from the return to normal currency conditions, or at any rate should not suffer, it was essential that, as the value of money increased, prices should quickly and spontaneously adjust themselves. As the pound sterling rose, prices should have fallen, but they did not do so. The revaluation of the pound undoubtedly caused wholesale prices to drop from 100 in 1924 to 70.7 in the third quarter of 1930, or about 30 per cent., but retail prices, and above all, wages—the primary element of cost—were still fixed at a different level. The reduction in retail prices was only from 100 to 89.3, or scarcely 11 per cent., while wages declined only from 100 to 98.2, an insignificant drop of 1.8 per cent.

Thus the fiscal policy keeps the pound sterling at one level, in spite of the fact that the cost of living and wages are pegged at another. As wholesale prices in a free-trade country are sensitive to international conditions, they have followed more closely the changes in the value of money; whereas retail prices and wages, being more national and political, are completely out of adjustment. The difference of 19 points between the wholesale and retail indices, and the 28 points between wholesale prices and wages, demonstrates the lack of flexibility of the social organism, arising from its failure to function normally. It is the still unpaid ransom of the war, and also the inevitable result of an unhealthy social policy, which is choking the British system. Under a *régime* of complete Free Trade, a state of equilibrium would have been quickly restored at home as well as abroad—but we must not forget that in the British structure *laissez-faire* belongs to the past.

This hardening of the arteries is peculiar to Western democracies, and particularly to England. Another characteristic of periods of confusion when monetary adjustments are taking place, is the dif-

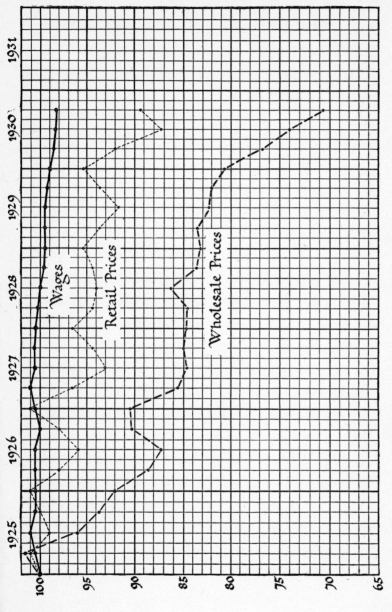

INDEX FIGURES FOR WHOLESALE PRICES, RETAIL PRICES AND WAGES

[1924 = 100]

ferent degree of sensitiveness of the various kinds of prices. During a period of deflation, this takes the form of sluggishness, such as has been experienced in England since 1921 and especially since 1925. A dual *régime* has thus arisen, in which currency used for international purposes has a greater purchasing power than that used for the home trade. This puts a premium on imports and a brake on exports. Manufacturing costs, owing to inertia, always tend to lag behind and remain at higher levels, and these circumstances inevitably sterilize a considerable part of the great efforts already made to improve technique and rationalize British industries.

The current against which the British are struggling is so strong, that all the energy in the world could hardly make headway against it. In international competition they are continually handicapped, since as producers they must operate on the higher level of domestic costs, while as exporters they must meet the lower world prices. This fact alone is sufficient to prevent their industries from exporting profitably, and at the same time it leaves their defenceless home market open to the dumping of foreign imports. This is a fatal reversal of the position of 1860, when everything tended to reduce British costs to a minimum.

With her economic structure thus mortgaged, England more than any other country fears any accentuation of the present tendency towards lower world prices, due to the rise in the value of gold. The more international price levels drop, the more difficult it becomes for her to adjust her own prices, owing to their inertia. A fall in world prices necessitates a reduction in costs, but England realizes that she cannot cut down wages, debts, or taxes. The more the gulf widens, the more she feels the weight of these rigid elements in her economic system. Let us not forget that when the pound succeeded in rejoining the dollar in 1925, it was to a great extent because the latter also had lost about a third of its purchasing power in comparison with pre-War levels. If the United States had gone in for a more accentuated policy of deflation, and had by this means raised the value of its money more quickly, England might not have been able to follow suit. Now that gold is tending to regain its pre-War value, this policy may prove to be an intolerable burden. This explains why England makes little attempt to conceal her desire for world inflation, which would result from a more intensive and concerted use of the gold supply. Raising prices in this way would ease the strain; here again we note that British instinct to change others rather than themselves.

We are therefore forced to the conclusion that though England alone among the European belligerents saved her currency by intense Budget energy and fiscal patriotism, the effort involved has proved too great a strain. She is bearing a load of debt that is too heavy; she is actually paying her creditors twenty shillings in the pound, while France is paying hers only twenty centimes in the franc.

England has achieved a state of financial equilibrium, but not an economic balance. The last word, however, has not yet been said, for if the pound is kept at the present level and the financial prestige of the nation is maintained, it may cost England her financial power, since that power is based on, and is inseparable from, a prosperous industry. An ingrained instinct caused the Government, rightly or wrongly, to consider restoring the currency as an essential duty, but in the last analysis it is industry which has to pay for saving the pound sterling. This is a clear example of the diversity of national interests which occurs when the economic machine is out of adjustment.

England believed that if she followed time-honoured methods, she would be able to emerge from the War and liquidate her financial situation without a surgical operation. In view of the exceptional circumstances, was this not excessive national pride? Also, she has not had a fresh start, like those who have gone through the bankruptcy court.

2. INDUSTRIAL EQUIPMENT AND ORGANIZATION

Britain's difficulties are aggravated by the old-fashioned conditions existing in certain industries. The principal nations of Western Europe, as well as the United States, have renewed their equipment to a great extent since the War. France was more or less forced to do so owing to the necessity of reconstructing her devastated areas; under other circumstances, possibly, she might not have done so. However that may be, Continental industry emerged rejuvenated, while England continues to congratulate herself on her thousand years of unbroken tradition. Perhaps she is wrong, for under certain circumstances it is better to pull everything up by the roots and start afresh.

In this respect British industry is like a virgin forest, where old decaying trees are surrounded by young saplings. Certain branches of industry have made remarkable technical progress during and since the War, but in others one still finds machines for which the proper place is a science museum. These machines are obsolete, almost useless, but they are kept, because in England they like to preserve everything.

The heavy industries, especially coal, iron, and steel, continue to use equipment which is frankly out of date. The coal industry works many pits which, technically, must be classed amongst the most antiquated in Europe. There is comparatively little mechanical extraction: wooden pit-props are still used, and the utilization of by-products, so important today, has progressed very slowly. Antediluvian coke ovens still function, and at most only about 25 per cent. of the coal is washed mechanically, whereas in Germany the figure is 80 per cent. and in France 85 per cent.

We find the same obsolete methods in entire branches of the iron and steel industry. Apart from certain ultra-modern works constructed during the War, the majority of the blast furnaces are still of very mediocre capacity in comparison with up-to-date practice; while the steel mills require decided remodelling if they are to be run on modern lines. One receives a general impression of worn-out equipment, in spite of certain remarkable exceptions. In the nineteenth century the engineers of the world came to England to learn the latest technical methods, but today they go to America or Germany, never to Durham, Northumberland, or South Wales.

Why this decadence? It cannot be lack of technical ability, for English engineers, taken individually are certainly efficient. They often have decided mechanical genius, and so have many of the foremen and workmen. They draw up plans for remodelling the machinery, and reorganizing the works, but only too often the owners will not listen. In times of prosperity the owners, who were accustomed to making money easily with their old equipment, could see no reason to change. They would always be prosperous, they thought, for is there not a special Providence that looks after the English? Now that things are going wrong, plant renovation is again postponed, but this time for different reasons. Confidence in the future of British industry has partially disappeared, and the boards of directors, inspired and often controlled by the banks, are tempted to declare that their capital would bring in a greater return if invested abroad. As a result, capital is turning away from certain industries, and it is difficult to raise sufficient funds for even the most urgently needed equipment.

The English always have a strong sense of duty. Englishmen are naturally loyal and generous, which has an important effect on the social aspect of manufacturing. For example, the social side of the factory is usually well organized, the social clubs are comfortable; to French eyes almost luxurious. The owners feel that the workmen must be humoured and their leisure supervised, so a considerable programme of expenditure is often agreed to. Strenuous efforts have been made during the past ten years to improve the workmen's dwellings, although in many cases it might have been more advantageous to reduce the man-power and construct fewer houses. All this adds to the cost of production.

Obsolete equipment is only one aspect of the depression, for the organization of industry itself is also at fault. In structure the basic industries, though not necessarily the others, still follow the main outline drawn up in the nineteenth century,

but that does not necessarily mean that it is bad—
on the contrary. Still, even though it made the fortunes of four generations, it is certainly not adapted
to the changing conditions of the present time.

In the nineteenth century everything was easy,
and industry developed naturally, growing daily in
stature like a boy. There was then no need to study
the relationship of each branch of industry in the
general picture. No one worried about such things,
for was there not a God to look after everything in
England, or at any rate to look after every Englishman? Progress was haphazard, for every one at-
tended to his own affairs and competed mercilessly
with his rivals. The individualism of the mid-Vic-
torians, their religion of *laissez-faire,* their clear
and simple conception of the freedom of competition, all lent itself to the working out of a system
which, in truth, produced a fine spirit of emulation.
Nevertheless, when there arose elsewhere a type of
national industry, collectively organized and with
military discipline, England still plodded along in
her same old rut. Although the momentum of success at first prolonged the era of profit, it eventually
became dangerous, as it seemed to justify individ-
ualistic habits and obsolete methods. Thus *laissez-*

faire, once the watchword of progress and initiative, became a lifeless parrot phrase, purposelessly repeated.

The coal industry, considered in the light of modern ideas, is typical of the irrational organization in Britain. In England the landowner is also the proprietor of the subsoil; hence a mining system that is entirely different from the French plan of concessions. In England the mining leases are now often of limited duration, and if they are not renewed on expiration the works erected by the lessee become the property of the landowners. One can appreciate that the lessee is unwilling to risk tying up capital for a long period, and that this causes the industry to remain in a very scattered state. In England there are 1400 independent coal producers operating 2000 pits, whereas in France we have 130 companies with 600 pits, and in Westphalia a dozen companies control nine-tenths of the production.

As is to be expected, instead of concentrating on the better pits, each English coalowner obstinately insists on working his own property, no matter how poor it may be. Every one works short time, and the burden weighs equally on all. The existence of semi-mediaeval pits, which are just able to carry on, acts as a drag on the whole industry, and injures the good pits which are equipped with the latest inventions. The inevitable result is maximum cost of production all round. So long as times were prosperous no one thought about reforms, for they did not appear to be urgent. Now that money is being lost every one is too discouraged, and the depression has created a sort of paralysis. Fresh capital is needed, but who wants to throw good money after bad? Sacrifices will have to be made, but who wants to do the sacrificing?

In view of the loss of the foreign markets, a collective selling organization is needed, but how can unity of action be obtained from hundreds of separate companies which have never co-operated in the past? Even now, when they are on the very brink of the precipice, intervention has had to come from outside the industry, for the Coal Mines Act of August 1930 at last forces them to collaborate.

The cotton industry is equally attached to the methods of the past. Its organization has scarcely changed since the second half of the last century: there are the same subdivisions into water-tight compartments—spinners, weavers, finishers, and

merchants—the same mulish individualism which
refuses to allow the necessary amalgamations, the
same childish conservatism which many consider a
virtue, the same belief that "Old England will pull
through somehow." In this case depression is caused
more by the antiquated system as a whole than by
the state of the plant. Some of the finest and most
modern mills in the world are to be found in Lancashire, but unfortunately they are being dragged
down to ruin with the rest. The fall in world prices,
together with the difficulty of lowering the cost of
production, and the merciless competition in the
home market between too many firms all cutting
each other's throats in their struggle for existence,
has in the end brought a whole section of the industry virtually to a state of bankruptcy.

What is needed is a general reorganization, which
will take into account the new conditions in manufacturing and world competition. The period of
scattered individualism has passed. To succeed today it is necessary to work with large units which
will assure effective co-operation, not merely within
any one section of the industry, but also with the
various other sections. For example, the finishers,
who made the first move, have proved that salvation

lies in this direction. There are, however, 700 spinning and 1200 weaving companies in Lancashire! The 700 managers of these spinning companies and the 1200 managers of these weaving companies, and Heaven knows how many others besides, are naturally afraid of reorganization, as its first effect would be to abolish a great many of their executive posts. The experience of the last three years shows that the cotton industry is having great difficulty in its attempt to reform. Here, again, the impulse must come from without, from the creditor banks or even from the Bank of England itself. This is a severe humiliation for Lancashire, which, far from depending on London, was once the guiding spirit of the entire economic policy of the nation.

These two typical examples show that the reorganization of the industry on national lines is not at present compatible with British genius. In Germany and France the principal branches of manufacturing have centralized organizations that are empowered to speak in international discussions on behalf of the industry as a whole. In this respect the English are decidedly behindhand. When foreign interests wish to get into contact with them they often do not know with whom to treat, and at times they find they are conferring with delegates who have insufficient powers. On various occasions this fact has made the entry of British industry into international cartels extremely difficult.

The old individualism, which in the nineteenth century was a source of strength, has now become a serious obstacle against which the champions of reorganization are doggedly struggling. In a speech at the Royal Colonial Institute in April 1928 the late Lord Melchett said: "The unit of production is too small and too feeble. To any man gifted with common sense and practical experience, it is evident that it is easier to discuss business when one speaks in the name of the whole industry instead of representing only one enterprise." During the past few years this man exercised a direct and powerful influence on the problem of industrial reorganization of his country, trying to make it conform with the needs of the times. It must be admitted that he brought to this task a spirit and traditions that were not strictly English.

Once again we are obliged to admit that during the present period of economic development the initiative no longer comes from England.

3. THE EMPLOYERS' ATTITUDE

British prestige in the last century was built up by an aristocracy of business men and statesmen, the former drawn from the middle, and the latter from the upper classes. The co-operation of these two groups overcame all obstacles. Unfortunately, once the industrialists became wealthy, they wished to penetrate into society, so instead of putting their sons into the business they sent them to the schools and universities where the statesmen had been trained. Shorn of its leaders, industry eventually rested on its laurels, and its progressive spirit died down to mere conservatism.

The outlook of the average industrialist has changed little during the past few generations; suffice it to say that he is simply a middle-class Englishman, insular and imbued with all the prejudices of his class. He clings to the old British idea that discipline and practical experience are better than technique. Talk with any of the English schoolmasters and you will invariably find that their aim is summed up in the formula: "We wish to turn out gentlemen." In other words, in their scale of values, they put character before business ability, and certainly before science. Thus, though the English may talk about rationalization—it is fashionable at present, just as in 1890 it was the thing to discuss technical education on the German model—yet the idea of rationalization is really foreign to them, and one sometimes wonders if they genuinely believe in it, or whether their talk is merely a veneer. Possibly they prefer to believe in their lucky star! They know that they make mistakes, and they are resigned to make plenty more, but in their innermost hearts they believe that they will muddle through, for after all that is what they were taught at school.

This easy-going attitude explains why the British business man so often lets himself be outdistanced by more aggressive and more capable rivals. He no longer fits into Keynes' description as "the feverishly active and alert figure of the classical economists, who never missed a chance of making a penny if it were humanly possible, and who was always in a state of stimulus up to the limit of his capacity." Today he deliberately takes life easy, and at times is almost "too proud to fight." He seems to be suffering from a lack of vitality.

French captains of industry, who go to England to discuss with their opposite numbers the various problems common to international production, have almost always brought back the same impression. They were not dealing with men of technical ability, or even of a general culture equal to their own. Foreign engineers, visiting England to study conditions, report the same thing. The managers of factories and the engineers whom they meet are usually not highly educated men, trained in the public schools, but rather specialists with no general background. Conversation with them is uninteresting; the problems discussed at the table or during their leisure hours are commonplace. Their outlook is often that of superior foremen who have risen in the world.

It must be admitted that since the War conditions have been changing, for the young men of the ruling classes are turning more and more towards industry. Cambridge is producing a fine body of engineers who possess both technical skill and culture, while at the same time the new provincial universities are exerting a steadily increasing influence. At these institutions, where the canker of sport is not allowed to overshadow everything else, they are turning out trained minds in tune with modern thought. If England will only rely on these new tech-

nicians, instead of choosing her leaders from the
sons and nephews of the present directors, from
those who bring capital into the business, or even
from clever, active foreigners, then we may look
for a social transformation of the utmost importance.

In a sense this transformation may come too late,
so slowly, indeed, that England will have meanwhile
been outdistanced by Germany, the United States,
and France. It is now over thirty years since the
French *bourgeoisie* partially abandoned the military
and administrative careers which had attracted them
for a century, and instead turned many of the best
brains of the country towards industry and Big
Business. England was possibly obeying a fundamental instinct in directing her leading minds into
political careers during the last two hundred years,
for the importance of her international relations
would have counselled this course. Nevertheless, the
immense complexity of modern industrial problems
will in future necessitate the choice of more highly
trained leaders in the business world.

Englishmen do not give the impression of decadence in this respect; in fact, quite recently they have
proved themselves capable of organizing new indus-

tries with the finest possible technique. When they are ploughing fresh ground they do it well, at times extremely well. It is only when they get into the rut of a routine that they are lulled to sleep by a fatal conservatism which they usually describe as tradition. This is as much a question of education as of character, which means that great changes are possible, and may prove to be necessary, in the outlook of the nation itself. Their pride in being practical rather than logical, the famous policy of "muddling through," the idealistic standards of the playing-fields of Eton, where, according to Wellington, the Battle of Waterloo was won—these things did well enough so long as England owed her success largely to her geographical position and mineral wealth.

Today this phase is over, and it is becoming steadily more difficult for England to maintain her position in the midst of unbridled competition, without the constantly sharpened weapons of superior organization and technique. The day of luck and lazy expedients is past. In war, in industry, in world-wide economic rivalry of every kind, it is no longer possible to succeed by relying on tradition alone. What is needed is brains and ability, both in touch with the last word in progress.

4. LABOUR

Finally, there has been a decided decline in the output of labour. There is no doubt about the excellent qualities of honesty, loyalty, and decent living, as well as the skill of the British workman, but the fact remains that he has been accustomed to and still clings to a wage level which is no longer compatible with the depressed state of industry.

Between 1914 and 1920 the British wage level rose from an index of 100 to 170-80. In 1929 the Ministry of Labour estimated it at from 170 to 175, and for 1930, Mr. Bowley, the well-known statistician of the London School of Economics, puts the figure at 178, showing that there has been no reduction from the peak figures of the post-War boom, and he also states that the reduction from the 1924 figure was only 1.80 per cent. Actually, instead of remaining stationary or declining, real wages have increased above the maximum of 1920, because wholesale prices have dropped from 325 to 122, and retail prices from 275 to 154. When he is employed, a workman is therefore as well off as he was in 1914, probably better; in 1914 he was consid-

erably better off than he was in 1900. In spite of
the past ten years of depression and unemployment,
the workingman has succeeded in maintaining an
exceptionably favourable wage level, which he is
now endeavouring to consolidate.

All workers are not equally favoured, for un-
skilled labour has benefited more than skilled, while
the sheltered domestic trades, not being subjected
to international competition, have profited. The export trades have had to adjust themselves more to
foreign levels, and therefore their workers have not
entirely maintained the increases acquired between
1914 and 1920.

The contrast between the wages of these two
categories is striking. In the first category, in 1929
bricklayers had an index of 178, day labourers in the
building trade 200, railway porters 230, skilled rail-
waymen 190, type-setters 207, bakers 213, and fur-
niture-makers 185 to 195. In the second category,
however, we find Northumberland coal-miners with
120, Welsh coal-miners with 135, engineering day
labourers with 183, but skilled mechanics with 151,
textile workers with 150, and skilled workmen in
the shipyards with 142. Thus, in trades which are
sheltered from foreign competition day labourers

get about 50s. a week and artisans from 70s. to 75s., whereas in the other class day labourers get about 40s. and specialists from 55s. to 60s. Since retail prices are about 50 per cent. to 60 per cent. higher than in 1914, the above figures indicate that some trades are better off and others are worse. However, according to Mr. Bowley, the average improvement in real wages between 1914 and 1929 was 17 per cent.

England is proud of this increase in her standard of living. The Press and the politicians never tire of congratulating themselves, and of comparing it with the poverty and mediocrity of the Continental nations. European wages, they say, mean starvation and slavery. Foreign competition is unfair, and Britain should not be asked to contend with it. The British workman has better food and clothing, is better housed and entertained, and has more leisure. Naturally this is expensive, but no one dreams of asking him to change his standards. His dignity is at stake. In short, the country has raised itself to a level where it is obliged to break away from the pressure of international competition. It insists that the national system should continue to function with no reduction in the standards that have been ac-

quired. America reasons the same way, but then
America is America.

We must, of course, make certain reservations
when discussing the real value of this famous standard of living. The English workman spends freely,
chiefly because he is not clever at organizing his life.
His wife is also somewhat lacking in *savoir-faire*.
She does not take a keen delight in shopping economically, nor does she pride herself on her cooking,
and the way in which she brings up her children is
open to criticism. She is honest and loyal, but slip-
shod, and her household often lives on canned goods
and prepared foods. As a housekeeper she has no
sense of, nor delight in, economy as we have in
France, and therefore she requires higher wages to
maintain a very ordinary standard. Do not imagine
that the French workman, though he receives less
than half as much money, lives only half as well.
This English standard of living means, to a certain
extent, the right to live shiftlessly without exertion,
and at the same time to be well paid for doing so.

Irrespective of what the workman does with his
wages, there is no doubt that they weigh heavily on
industry, although high wages do not necessarily
mean high costs of production, since it is quite pos-

sible for output to increase as rapidly as the rate of wages. In England, however, neither equipment nor organization have progressed in proportion to real wages, while the workers themselves, imbued with old ca'canny prejudices, are stolidly opposed to mechanical progress. Under such conditions the cost of wages per unit of production has increased instead of being reduced. This is not only true of the sheltered industries where no sacrifice has been asked from the workers, but also of the exporting industries, where wages have been greatly reduced. The high level of domestic prices, which is closely linked to the general wage level, increases every element in the cost of production. The cost of the exported article is as much affected as is the cost of the article which is for home consumption, by such factors as the expensive coat which the workman wears, the gas and electricity in his home, the costly spare parts with which the management repairs the machines, and the crushing freight charges on all imports and shipments. No industry can escape from this expensive atmosphere.

In the United States although costs are even higher this obstacle is overcome by superior methods of mass production, against which England competes with difficulty. But in certain other countries, as for example Continental Europe and Asia, everything is cheaper, including wages. Here again England cannot compete, especially against those whose equipment has been renewed. True, British wages have always been higher than those of the rest of Europe, but the spread has, if anything, been increased. According to the Ministry of Labour, the comparison in 1927 was as follows:

COMPARISON OF ENGLISH AND FOREIGN WAGES

England	100
United States	175
Canada	150-155
Denmark	105-110
Holland	85-90
Germany	65-70
France	55-60
Belgium	50-55
Italy, Austria, Poland	45-50

Thus even such serious competitors as France, Belgium, and Poland pay their workmen on an average only one-half of what the British workman receives, and at the same time the plant on the Continent is not necessarily inferior to the British. Detailed reports of practically all industries lead to the same conclusion, namely that, independent of other factors, the lower wages on the Continent have placed British industries in a manifestly inferior position. One can quote scores of examples, but the following will serve our purpose:

According to Mr. Clarence Smith, President of the Consett Iron Company, wages in the French steel industry are only 50 per cent. of the British, and in Belgium, Luxembourg and Czechoslovakia, they are lower still.[1]

Mr. James Hardy, at the annual general meeting of Fras. Hinde & Hardy, silk manufacturers, in August 1930, stated that wages in Lyons were only 40 per cent. to 50 per cent. of the corresponding British wages.

According to documents submitted in 1930 by the International Labour Office at a technical conference on working conditions in the coal mines, the relative wage level of miners was as follows: England, 100; Ruhr, 75; France, 65; Poland, 50.

The evil from which England is suffering is that a whole section of the population is overpaid for its services, while the profits on capital are correspondingly diminished.

That is the real cause of the trouble. When prices

[1] *The Times,* "City Notes," 21st June 1930.

started to drop in 1921 owing to the rise of the
pound sterling, nominal wages should have declined
in proportion. If this adjustment had taken place,
real wages would have been left intact, and the cost
of production would have been relieved by the
amount of the reduction. As England was not willing to reform, each increase in real wages actually
became a direct increase in manufacturing costs,
until a staggering burden was laid on the shoulders
of the nation.

The malady arises from many causes, all of which
can be traced to a single germ. In a healthy economic
structure, wages and prices, being retarded only by
normal inertia, adjust themselves without difficulty. But in England, there is also the social organization to contend with. The entire economic
structure is frozen. No other community today
is suffering to such an extent from this paralysis. Certain compartments in the national structure
are isolated from the levelling influence of economic
laws. The flexibility of retail prices is also considerably hampered, whereas in the case of wages the
greater part seems to be rigidly pegged. The trade
unions have imposed their point of view, and now
every increase in wages, with the social progress in-

volved, is considered a moral conquest for Labour that must not be given up at any price.

As a result the workers have lost sight of the fact that wages, output, and profits, are all closely related. They contend that the nation owes them a certain wage, and that it is the owner's duty to pay it as best he can. England may be going through a serious crisis, but that does not move them in the least.

In France we see nothing shameful in cutting down our standard of living, but to the Anglo-Saxon it is humiliating. This trade union point of view is shared by the whole country, except, of course, the employers. There seems to be a tacit understanding that the people should live as comfortably today as they did in 1914, in spite of the War, and in spite of the present depression. When the employer says that this is impossible, and that his wages bill is crushing him, the workman replies, "Rationalize, or reduce your profits!" Each class tries to throw the responsibility on the other. Public opinion is with the working-classes in this dispute, as is to be expected in a working-class community, and no politician, not even a Conservative, dares oppose this unorganized but irresistible attitude. The standard of living theme is emphasized quite as much in the speeches of the Conservatives as in those of Labour. The dignity of the British people, they maintain, is at stake.

5. THE POISON OF UNEMPLOYMENT

High wages are the direct cause of unemployment. If wages are definitely fixed at a level which does not allow manufacturers to make a profit, then one section of the community must necessarily be out of work. Since the War British wages have not been adapted to meet the fall in prices, and consequently the increase in real wages has brought with it a corresponding increase in unemployment. In 1925 this fundamental law was analyzed for the first time by M. Jacques Rueff, who proved it with startling clarity in the chart which is here reproduced.[1] The extent to which the system is blocked by its lack of elasticity is indicated with mathematical precision.

Unemployment is not a cause but a result. It has, however, been aggravated by remedies applied as the official policy of the country during the past ten

[1] Jacques Rueff, "Les Variations du Chomage en Angleterre," *Revue Politique et Parlémentaire,* 10 décembre, 1925.

years, remedies which have now poisoned the whole
system and paralyzed certain organs.

In England unemployment does not arise from
any "unemployability" on the part of labour itself.
According to the Ministry of Labour, male employability is regular in 66.9 per cent. of cases, sufficient
in 21.9 per cent., bad in 4.9 per cent., and totally
insufficient in only 2 per cent.[1] It is generally admitted that work could be found for many more
people if the rate of remuneration were sufficiently
lowered. Stated in these simple terms, the problem
and the solution are perfectly clear; in the long run
every one would benefit, for there would be less unemployment and fewer factories running on part
time. Nominal wages would be lower, but the number receiving them would be greater and the weekly
wage bill also would be larger, which would increase
the total purchasing power of the nation.

The truth of this reasoning is perfectly obvious,
but the hostility of the trade unions is inflexible, and
in general public opinion agrees with them. They
prefer high wages with unemployment, to lower

[1] Ministry of Labour Investigation into the personal circumstances
and industrial history of a 1 per cent. sample of the claimants to unemployment benefit in the first week of April 1927; 4.3 per cent. are
not placed in the above categories.

wages with the unemployed reabsorbed, for lower wages mean a reduction in the standard of living. In a word, England would rather support indefinitely a million unemployed than reduce wages. As this attitude is firmly rooted in the British mind, any practical study of the present crisis must take into consideration the methods of distributing the dole. To all intents and purposes unemployment is accepted and supported, until it has now become a permanent characteristic of modern England.

Although unemployment insurance dates back to 1912, it did not function on a large scale until after the War, and it is only since then that its main aspects have been altered, and it has developed into its present form. When the system was originally conceived by experts of the Board of Trade, it was a genuine insurance, having a strict relationship between the premiums paid by the workers and the employers on the one hand, and the indemnity received on the other. Although a contribution was paid by the State, the system was contractual and confined to a few industries only. The limits were prudently fixed, and the beneficiaries were entitled to only petty sums compared with their normal wages. At the end of fifteen weeks assistance stopped automatically.

After the Armistice, and especially in 1920, Eng-

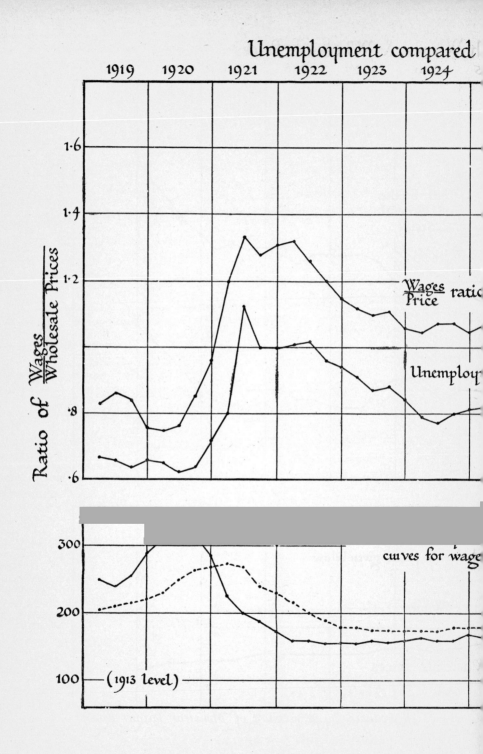

1919 1920 1921 1922 1923 1924

Ratio of Wages / Wholesale Prices

1·6

1·4

1·2

·8

·6

Wages / Price ratio

Unemploy

300

200

100 — (1913 level)

curves for wage

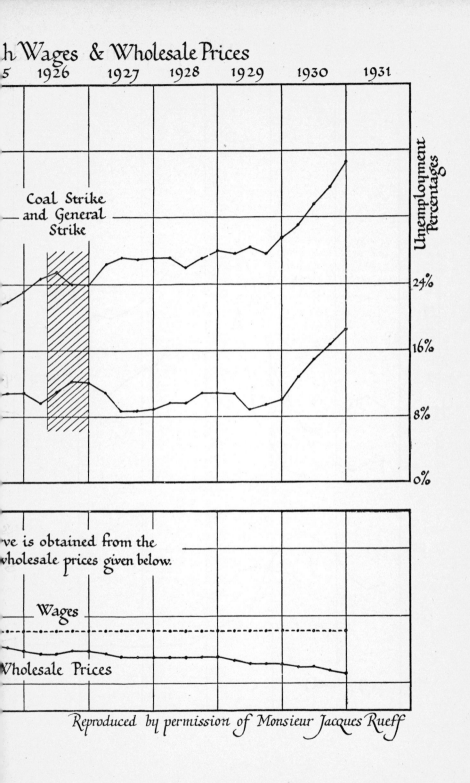

h Wages & Wholesale Prices

5   1926   1927   1928   1929   1930   1931

Coal Strike
and General
Strike

Unemployment
Percentages

24%

16%

8%

0%

ve is obtained from the
wholesale prices given below.

Wages

Wholesale Prices

Reproduced by permission of Monsieur Jacques Rueff

land was overwhelmed by the violence of the economic crisis. By the 1920 law unemployment insurance was extended to include all workers except domestic servants and agricultural labourers, but an effort was still made to maintain the original principles. Little by little, however, owing to the irresistible pressure of circumstances, an entirely different conception was evolved. In 1921 a special allowance for dependants was added, and the share borne by the Treasury correspondingly increased. In 1924 the time limit for receiving assistance was abolished by the Labour Government then in power. From then on aid was given automatically as long as the worker was without employment, and naturally there was no further hope of a financial balance.

The years passed. Unemployment became a tradition, and the safeguards against abuse were whittled down by the persistence of the demagogues. Originally, in order to receive assistance, the worker had to prove that he had been "genuinely seeking work but unable to obtain suitable employment." In 1930 another amendment was passed by the Labour Government, disqualifying the worker only if he had "refused without good cause suitable employment offered him by a Labour Exchange." He is no longer expected to look for work himself. The interpretation of the term "suitable employment" is so broad, that without being disqualified, a workman can refuse any post, even though he has the ability for it, if he thinks he has been offered less than the regular rate, or if the job is made available by a strike. If it pleases him he can refuse any job for which he has not been definitely trained, even though it is in a trade allied to his own.

The same amendment of 1930, with an entire lack of restraint, succeeded in removing the remaining obstacles against the squandering of public funds. The worker is no longer required to have paid a minimum of thirty contributions during the previous two years. The unemployed draw on the funds, but the Treasury has to make up the deficit. The rules stating how soon assistance can be received have also been relaxed. Although aid is not given for the first six days of unemployment, after that unemployment is not considered to have ceased, even though the worker may find casual employment for three days in the week.

By a similar evolution, the rate of benefit, both nominal and real, has steadily increased since 1912 when it was 7s. per week. Today a married man receives 17s. in addition to 9s. for his wife and 2s.

for each child. If he has five children, which is not unusual, he receives 36s. The municipalities can also augment the dole in various ways if they consider it insufficient. Up to 1929 there were Poor Law Guardians especially elected for this purpose, and they often gave a supplementary grant of 6s. or 7s. The increase in the dole can be fully appreciated only if the decline in prices since 1920 is taken into account. At that time each unemployed receives 15s., and retail prices were at an index of 275; today he receives 17s. and the index has fallen to about 150 —in other words, the indemnity has almost doubled. Here again, as in the case of wages, we find that during periods of falling prices, no steps have been taken to prevent the burden increasing automatically.

The result of this evolution is positively terrifying, for the system—if the term may still be used —has lost all actuarial basis. One can no longer honestly call it insurance, as it is tending to become public assistance, and the drag on the State finances is growing steadily heavier. True, the workers still give their weekly sums, but there is no relationship between what they pay and what they receive. The employers, on the other hand, are struggling under a far heavier obligation, for as there is no longer any elasticity in the system, their contribution remains fixed in spite of the decline in prices. In reality, the employer pays a tax on every man he hires, and the more active the industry, therefore, the greater the tax, although in practice the greater the activity the less the need for assistance. The solidarity existing between the various industries is increasing costs all round, for those that are prosperous are contributing to help those that are sick. The former pay out but receive no benefit, while the latter receive possibly ten times as much as they pay. When the number of unemployed rises above a certain figure, the financial equilibrium vanishes. The fund turns for help to the limitless purse of the State, and the Treasury makes an advance which it knows will never be repaid. The chasm is yawning wide, but the public does not seem to worry. Judging from the various enquiries that have been made, the country is resigned to have the dole frankly become State assistance without contribution from the beneficiaries.

The financial consequences are, nevertheless, not the most serious aspect. One can hardly exaggerate the economic and social evils arising from the chronic existence of a paid army of unemployed, whose numbers for the past ten years have never fallen below a million. This is sapping the strength of the nation morally even more than materially.

The most dangerous defect of the system is the spirit of complacency which it has created. A foreigner going to England expects to find an atmosphere of tragedy, but on the contrary he finds exactly the opposite. The English workman knows that when he loses his job, no matter what happens, he will not starve; he becomes a social *rentier,* living at the expense of the nation. His standard of living may be reduced, but he can still live, so he awaits with calm—often too much calm—the chance of further employment.

The employer also profits from the knowledge that a discharged workman will be cared for by the State, and he therefore does not hesitate to hire and discharge without rhyme or reason. Instead of making a serious effort to adjust their staffs to their needs, many employers have learned to take advantage of the existence of a permanent excess of man-power, and rather than try to save labour they draw at will from this reserve. Latent unemployment is thus definitely established and maintained, one might almost say encouraged. The fact that it may not be continuous, but is spread over several days of the week, scarcely alters its pernicious effect.

The management will sometimes arrange matters with the workers so that they lose as little as possible of their right to the dole, and often the men are not hired for more than three days running, so that they can still be legally considered unemployed. In the dockyards, the building trades, and several other fields of labour, these practices are common and even openly admitted. To take advantage of the dole may profit the individual, but it is ruining the nation.

The same security affects even the small trades-folk, who congratulate themselves that consumption will be steady, for their customers, whether they are in employment or not, will always have money to spend. The workman's credit, at least so far as immediate wants are concerned, has undoubtedly increased. As we shall see later, unemployment insurance and various other forms of public assistance have created for the masses a steady purchasing power, the effects of which are far from negligible.

The most dangerous and also the most subtle element of paid unemployment is the slow breaking down of the will to work. In certain cases it actually pays better to be idle, for the workman is better off. Taking everything into account, a man can often receive more from the dole and the Guardians than from working normally at his trade. According to the report of the Assistant General Inspector of the Ministry of Health, the following scandalous cases are cited:[1]

An engineer fitter from Southwark, aged 36 years, married and the father of five children, has been assisted almost continuously since 1925. He has received 43s. a week, and since the birth of his last child, 47s. If he worked at his trade he would earn 42s. for a 47-hour week. Case two: A carman from Southwark received in 1921 a wage of 41s. He had intermittent relief from 1922 to 1925, and since June 1925 had continuous out-relief at the rate of 45s. a week. The relieving officer reported the wife's statement that the man had been offered three days' work a week, but he did not accept it, "as they would have been out of pocket."

These extreme cases are due largely to the excessive generosity of the demagogue Guardians.

[1] *The Times,* 26th November 1927.

However, since many wages in England do not exceed 40s., and as the regular dole for a man with a family of five children amounts to 36s., there can obviously be little or no incentive to work in any case. When the employment offered is for part of the week only, it is naturally better to stay at home. In *The Times* of 11th October 1930 there appeared an announcement of the final closing down of the Dowlais Steel Works, which turned on to the street 2800 men. The article concludes as follows: "It is said that a certain proportion of the lower-paid men with large families will probably receive almost as much from the dole as they have done in wages."

Under such conditions it is easy to understand why the wage level has not declined, even during a long period of depression. Why should it decline, if it is to no one's interest to work at a lower rate? Nor is there any incentive to try a new trade, or even to accept new conditions of work in one's own line if they might not be quite so satisfactory. In 1930 the Lancashire cotton operatives refused to run eight looms at once, and the dole was there to back them up. The trade unions have been strengthened in this and other wage disputes. Strike-breakers and "scabs" are thus eliminated. This is one of the main reasons for the lack of harmony between wages and prices.

The dole is naturally insufficient for the normal upkeep of a family, and after a time various exceptional expenses for clothing and the house cannot be met. Such is the case in the little mining towns where the pits have been abandoned, and the people have been in want for some time. If a sort of communal life is organized, with the married children living with the parents and the younger ones already out at work, the dole received by part of the family, added to the wages received by the rest, together makes up sufficient income. The part played in the family budget by the dole is rather like taking in boarders. Eventually they are reconciled to a conception of life from which all sense of responsibility—one might say of dignity—has disappeared.

From being an insured worker who has paid his contribution, the unemployed tends to become a pauper, kept by the State. The "dole," a derogatory expression implying the humiliation of receiving alms, is eventually considered as a right, and is received without shame. There develops a spirit of mendicity, of which British history reveals traces in the past. Beggars stand, hat in hand, in the streets. Labour, too, is not above cadging in Parliament or elsewhere, especially if there is any question of fixing its status. According to Mr. W. A. Appleton, Secretary of the General Federation of Trades Unions, at the time of the General Strike in 1926 the workers "were chiefly interested in making new appeals for personal, local, national, or international charity. They did not hesitate to make fresh demands for their own benefit on the reserves of capital, although these were already insufficient for any industry which was anxious to bring itself up to date."

The moral fibre of the unemployed cannot resist either the life they are now leading, or the complacency with which it is accepted. A feeling of slackness pervades the atmosphere; inspectors report that they often find the inveterate unemployed stretched out in bed during the day. For these leftovers, hour follows hour with nothing to do except an occasional visit to the Labour Exchange to see if by any chance there is a job to be had. Finally, all effort, aptitude, and energy are benumbed.

The life of the nation goes on none the less, with a tranquillity and regularity that is most deceptive. The Government seems to fear this great body of idle men, and does what is urgent; it supports them, making sure that they remain calm, and are not driven to desperation. Foreign economists may argue that a policy of *laissez-faire* would soon put England on her feet again. This is the way they talk when they are outside the country. They need only go to England to realize that no politician dare make a direct attack on the dole; he would soon lose his seat.

Meanwhile, this multitude of unemployed try, with reason, to amuse themselves, and in this they have the tacit approval of the Government, which regards as useful diversions the cinema, athletics, and greyhound-racing, the latter being the latest craze. In England the love of sport acts like a drug on the masses. When it comes to football or racing, there seems to be a mutual understanding between the trade unionist and the aristocrat. Although the Government possibly does not realize it, this chloroform policy has succeeded in counteracting any germ of revolution in the unemployment crisis—it is the *"panem et circenses"* of the Romans!

Nevertheless, the presence of this dead member, which apparently is not being amputated, is poisoning the whole body politic. There is, indeed, "something rotten in the state of Denmark."

CHAPTER III

HIGH INDUSTRIAL COSTS— EXTERNAL CAUSES

I. CHANGES IN THE WORLD'S METHODS

THE various causes of industrial decadence analyzed in the last chapter can all be remedied by
England herself. Eventually, the lack of adjustment
between retail and wholesale prices will be ironed
out, and also the difference in purchasing power
between the pound sterling and foreign currencies.
Industrial equipment can and will be renewed; industry will be reorganized, continuing the process already begun; the working-class will learn the futil-
ity of costly and useless strikes; unemployment will
ultimately eliminate itself by emigration, as well as
by birth control, that spontaneous method by which
a social organism automatically adjusts itself. None
of these, however, can alone solve the problems of
high manufacturing costs, for the root causes are
independent of Britain herself, and she seems to be
struggling vainly against them.

More important even than the advent of rivals in every part of the world, is the far-reaching transformation which has taken place during the twentieth century in the conditions of industrial production.

In the past, coal was equivalent to industrial power, and a map of the coal basins in any country or continent was virtually a map of its manufacturing areas. Today this is only partially true. Though coal is still the main fuel, water-power and oil have become such important sources of energy that they are undermining its tyrannous supremacy. Moreover, it is no longer being used in the same way as before; indeed, it is no exaggeration to say that with the decline of the steam engine the coal age itself is becoming a thing of the past.

Oil and petrol are rapidly coming to the fore, especially in the domain of transport, which the nineteenth century imagined would always be reserved for coal. The motor-car and the aeroplane now belong entirely to petrol, and even shipping is beginning to discard the steam engine. The following table explains the situation:

THE WORLD'S TONNAGE CLASSIFIED

	1913	1930
Sailing ships	8.00%	2.30%
Steamships burning coal	88.90%	57.60%
Steamships burning fuel oil	2.65%	28.50%
Motor ships consuming Diesel oil	.45%	11.60%

It is apparent that there has been a decline of the steam engine in favour of the internal combustion engine, and at the same time a decline of coal in favour of fuel oil. Before the War 91.55 per cent. of the world's tonnage was propelled by steam, but the proportion has now fallen to 86.1 per cent. The decline of coal is even more accentuated, being from 88.9 per cent. to 57.6 per cent. The advent of the steamship with oil-fired boilers has now robbed coal of much of its domain. A survey of the tonnage under construction in 1930 indicates this loss of monopoly, and shows that the high seas have been virtually conquered by the internal combustion engine.

TONNAGE UNDER CONSTRUCTION

(September 1930)

Sailing ships	0.6%
Steamships (coal and oil)	38.8%
Motor ships	60.6%

If we study the total production of industrial power throughout the world, we see that the coal monopoly is disappearing in the same way. In 1927 coal accounted for 77 per cent. of the total energy, and if we include lignite, 79 per cent. We find that 15 per cent. came from oil, and 6 per cent. from water-power. By comparing these with pre-War figures, we see that oil and water-power have gained exactly what coal has lost, *i.e.* approximately 13 per cent. between 1913 and 1924. Coal is making little real progress, for between 1925 and 1929 the total mined increased by only 4 per cent., whereas oil production expanded by 24 per cent. and water-power by 40 per cent.

Herein lies an incontestable menace to the equilibrium of British trade, which depends to so great an extent on exports. In the nineteenth century it was an undoubted advantage for England to be able to feed her factories with coal obtained locally, there being no need to import or even transport fuel. This advantage still exists, but it is of less importance since many of England's rivals depend either on their own coal-fields, or on water-power, in which she is deficient. Many countries are gradually freeing themselves from the necessity of importing coal, and English exports are, in consequence, declining. The sale of bunker coal also is diminishing, for a steadily increasing number of ships are being designed for fuel oil, and therefore have no need of coal. It is possible to foresee a time at no distant date when coal will be transported only in the form of electrical or gaseous energy.

Under such conditions coal will cease to be so decisive a factor in the British carrying trade. Indeed, for some years an increasing number of ships have been leaving British ports in ballast. Consequently in working out the cost of freight the shipowner has no longer the same advantage as his predecessor, who was able to count on an assured profit by starting the voyage with a cargo of coal. Instead, the country must now import her oil; the merchant marine, the navy, aviation, and even the army itself depend almost entirely on fuel oil and petrol, neither of which are produced in Great Britain.

The fear voiced in the past by Stanley Jevons, that England would one day be obliged to import her fuel, is thus being partially realized. True, his prophecy has not been fulfilled exactly as he foresaw, for he was considering the exhaustion of the mines, and not the competition of a new source of power. The evil effects are identical, however, for in either case the result is a reduction in exports coincident with a forced increase in imports, with cost prices higher all round. The British, in consequence, are making every effort to produce synthetic oil, and are closely studying the use of pulverized fuel.

A century ago England had no difficulty in paying for her share of the Napoleonic Wars, thanks to the vigorous development of her coal basins and to the invention of the steam engine, which became her special prerogative. The losses in the last War could similarly have been met by a new utilization of natural forces in conformity with the needs and methods of the times,—but alas, to make use of natural forces one must possess them. England is blessed only with coal, with which, as she clearly realizes, her lot is indissolubly linked.

So the argument turns once again against nineteenth-century England, for today the chief factor in low-production costs is not so much the possession of power—whether coal, oil, or water—but rather the mass production of standardized articles for consumption in an enormous home market. For over ten years Henry Ford has been producing more cheaply than his European competitors, mainly because he has at his door 130 million potential customers, people who are themselves practically as standardized as the machines he sells them. True, he obtains his power and raw material under exceptionally favourable conditions, but the essence of his success is the tremendous volume of his output.

The whole international system of industry has been transformed by his methods. The export trade, especially, has changed in character, for it is no longer an essential and normal element as it was in the old countries of the last industrial phase. Instead, it has become a regulator, leading eventually and almost inevitably to dumping. Dumping does not necessarily mean a loss, and can be carried on permanently, for the profits obtained at home permit a new liberty of action abroad. The regularity of production, made possible by the relative stability of the home market, serves as a fly-wheel, any surplus under this new system being thrown upon the foreign market.

At the present time mass production is carried on under more favourable conditions in the United States than anywhere else in the world. As M. Paul

Morand observes, the world today must be considered in terms of continental masses, and that little island, England, once pre-eminent owing to circumstances now past and gone, is no longer particularly favoured. She is, in fact, caught between two fires. In 1866 Sir Charles Dilke, during his voyage round the world, noted the "defeat of the cheaper by the dearer peoples, the victory of the man whose food cost four shillings over the man whose food cost fourpence." England is now outdistanced quite as much by the dearer countries as by the cheaper. Among those with high wages, America surpasses her in both volume and organization; on the other hand, the low-wage countries often have ultra-modern machinery which outclasses the old-fashioned British equipment, constructed and planned as it was to meet the needs of a time when America scarcely existed, and when many of the young countries were only emerging from the chrysalis.

If present conditions had prevailed at the beginning of the nineteenth century, when the industrial system of modern England was being evolved, it is by no means certain that the most powerful manufacturing concentration in the world would have

been located on this little island on the edge of the
European continent. At any rate the combination
of circumstances most conducive to cheap industrial
production is no longer to be found in this part of
the world.

2. THE ALTERED CLIENTELE

It is not only the methods of production that have
changed, but also the types and quality of the
articles produced and sold. This change has come
about as the result of a veritable revolution in the
taste and requirements of the consumer, as compared with preceding generations. Possibly the reason for the alteration in the character of the consumption is the output of standardized articles in the
United States. Mankind is being transformed by
these standardized articles, be it in America, Argentina, or China, and this transformation is taking
place with terrifying rapidity. Thus the prosperous
industries of the twentieth century are not, and
could not possibly be, the ones which led in the nineteenth, unhappily for those who, being asleep, allowed themselves to be linked too closely with the
dusty past.

The requirements of the world today have greatly

changed. The demand for prime necessities such as food and normal clothing has decreased, in favour of things to satisfy desires that are obviously of secondary importance, even pure nonsense. Essentials are being systematically relegated to the background, while everything for the leisure hours is much in demand. Luxury, or at any rate imitation luxury, is popular—every one must have it. In the United States the French phrase, "de luxe," has become quite stereotyped. Ordinary clothing is superseded by fabrics considered more "de luxe" —less wool and cotton, but more silk, and ten times more artificial silk,—so the cotton trade suffers in consequence.

Meanwhile, a host of new expenses figure in every one's budget, expenses suggested by industries which seem almost to have sprung out of the blue, for twenty years ago they did not even exist. The world's consumption is now largely made up of an endless demand for automobiles, gramophones, radios, electrical gadgets, telephones, cinematographs, cameras, etc. There seems to be no end to the sale of articles for travel, sports, and gardening, and the profusion of illustrated magazines describing them is positively limitless. This phenomenon far exceeds the stimulus created by a boom period, and will probably outlive the passing effects of an economic depression. This is evidently one by-product of the spread of democracy among the masses, who, weary of restraint, are at last insisting on having their share in the good things of life. By diminishing the general sense of responsibility and thrift, and by suddenly revealing the profound instability of our age, the War hastened this evolution of humanity towards immediate gratification. Asia and Africa are rapidly following in the wake of America and Europe in this respect.

American industry was conceived, organized, and equipped in response to demands which it had itself created, and which it has to maintain at all costs. Modern man is so constructed that he is an ideal customer for these standardized articles, so it is on the American plan, not on the European plan, that the world is revising its conceptions and mode of life. It follows, as a result, that the demand for the so-called American products is absorbing an increasing share of the purchasing power of the international market. Traditional commercial currents and old-established businesses are being displaced, and an important part of the world's foreign trade is being diverted from its accustomed channels. The Argentine consumer, and even the Chinese consumer, are thinking today of motor cars, gramophones, and radios, instead of cotton fabrics, Sheffield cutlery, or British porcelain. The progress of the American export trade in all the newer markets is based on the sale of motor cars, cinema films, electrical equipment, radios, typewriters, office equipment and calculating machines, sewing machines, household utensils, refrigerators, agricultural implements, road-making machinery, oil-drilling equipment, and so on.

Naturally, there are still and there always will be purchasers for basic manufactured goods produced by the metal, cotton, and woollen trades, but these are no longer the star turns. Although they are still important, in fact essential, they have been the least prosperous since the War. The blue ribbon is now bestowed elsewhere, and countries which, by necessity or habit, are identified with these staple industries are liable to be out of date, and, to a certain extent, out of the running. They are losing the world's markets, and the wealth which once flowed to them is turning towards the new type of producer.

England has drifted into an unsatisfactory situation because her basic industries are exactly of this old-fashioned type; her export trade and her prosperity depended on iron and steel, cottons, woollens, and jute. In this sphere her products are excellent, honestly made, and justly renowned, but somewhat out of date. When the public wants something different, she replies, and with reason, that her articles are good, solid, and durable; the public answers that that is exactly what is wrong with them, for if they are to be fashionable they must not last too long. If we study any of the international markets, the Argentine, for instance, where British supremacy used to be traditional, we see clearly that England has not lost her clientele, but that the old type of trade has been replaced by a new one in which her share is small, either because she does not produce the specialty required, or because her salesmanship is not good enough.

This is the conclusion gathered from recent enquiries, such as the brilliant report made on British commerce in South America by Lord d'Abernon in 1930. One may say that the remedy lies with the manufacturer and salesman, for if so many others succeed, why not the English? It is true that many of the new types of articles, like motor cars, gramophones, electrical equipment, artificial silk, etc., are being made in England. But these are all mass produced, and moreover require a certain alacrity of invention and adaptation, which frankly is not part of the English genius. England can certainly succeed where others do, though perhaps not better than the rest. The United States, borne along by the rising tide, works under the aegis of mass production, as she is undoubtedly better suited for this task, and is steadily capturing markets which hitherto have been almost an English monopoly.

Once again, in this new century, which is so different from its predecessor, circumstances have not upheld England's leadership, and even the utmost ability is incapable of maintaining it. The tide is flowing in another direction. What, then, is to become of England's economic position, which has always been based on the hypothesis that she will retain the first place?

CHAPTER IV

BRITAIN'S ECONOMIC EQUILIBRIUM

I. BALANCE OF TRADE

THE steadily growing deficit in the trade balance of post-War Britain is one of the most serious features in her economic situation.

BRITISH TRADE BALANCE

(Millions of Pounds)

	Imports	Exports	Re-exports	Total Exports	Balance	Exports Per cent.
1913	769	525	110	635	—134	82
1920	1933	1334	223	1557	—134	80
1921	1086	703	107	810	—276	74
1922	1004	720	104	824	—180	82
1923	1098	768	119	887	—211	81
1924	1277	801	140	941	—336	74
1925	1323	773	154	927	—396	70
1926	1242	652	126	778	—464	63
1927	1219	709	123	832	—387	68
1928	1197	723	120	843	—354	70
1929	1222	730	110	840	—382	69

It is true that even before 1914 British trade had always shown an adverse balance, for that is the

normal condition of a rich, old, creditor country.
Since the War the proportion of imports paid for
by exports has appreciably diminished, the figure
having declined from 80 per cent. to the 70 per cent.
level, where it seems to be fixed. This is due to the
fact that exports have not increased, whereas imports have expanded considerably. If instead of ex-
amining the nominal value of the figures in pounds
sterling, we estimate the volume they represent, we
see clearly the dissimilarity between the trends followed by the export and the import trades. Expressed in terms of 1913 prices, the volume of exports has decreased by about 20 per cent. while imports have increased by at least the same amount.
Even between 1924 and 1929, the volume of imports has risen from an index of 100 to 114.1, in
spite of an apparent reduction in the nominal figures.

Undeniably, the monetary policy is partly responsible, for as we have already seen, it is stimulating
imports and putting a brake on exports. Inflation
would have had an entirely different effect. Nevertheless, in spite of this reduction in exports, the English continue to fill their wants from abroad as
freely and generously as ever. According to authori-

ties on the subject, the masses have maintained and even improved their pre-War standard of living, a victory which the Government of the day, irrespective of party, never fails to point out. Public opinion is particularly proud of such progress.

We have already shown the increase that has taken place in real wages, and this has been considerably supplemented by the social services, including various insurances and pensions of every kind. Since the proportion of the family budget devoted to current expenses has increased to the detriment of savings, it follows that although the national revenue may not have risen, the total resources at the disposal of the masses is as great if not greater than before the War. This is a triumph for the people. The upper classes are preyed upon and their wealth reduced, while democracy blossoms out and congratulates itself on its material progress.

It would be absolutely erroneous to picture England as miserable and depressed. The *per capita* consumption of bread and meat may have gone down slightly, but the demand for farm produce, vegetables, tea, and sugar, has increased. Housing has improved, thanks to an intensive programme of construction of workmen's dwellings, while the general development of amusements of every kind has been very great. For the period of 1909-13 home-grown food amounted to 59.5 per cent. of the total consumed, but for 1924-28 this figure fell to 56.7 per cent.[1] Obviously, imports must have expanded, even without taking into account the increase in population.

For a long time it was believed that this rise in foreign purchases, combined with the persistent stagnation in exports, was only a passing phase. This feeling was natural at the time of the Armistice, for it was to be expected that the World War would produce vigorous fluctuations, but as the disorder is continuing, one now wonders whether it may not be permanent, and if it possibly signals a new order of things. In a word, England will evidently have to learn to carry on with a lower volume of exports, but in so doing is she not courting disaster?

2. BALANCE OF PAYMENTS

The terrifying adverse balance in British trade has not failed to impress public opinion on the Con-

[1] A. W. Flux, *Proceedings of the Royal Statistical Society,* "Our Food Supply Before and After the War," 17th June 1930.

tinent, where it has been interpreted with considerable pessimism, owing to the traditional mercantile outlook of these countries. In Europe, for the past few years, we have been daily preparing a first-class funeral for England—and yet she is not necessarily down and out. Except during depressions such as 1929-30 or in periods of social upheaval, one can discern a certain balance in her economic structure —at any rate this is the opinion of the great majority of the English themselves.

The Board of Trade publishes annually a conservative estimate of the country's balance sheet, which is usually accepted as a general basis for discussion.

Although this estimate does not take into consideration the movements of capital, it gives a partial reply to the essential question: "How does post-War Britain pay for her imports?" Evidently she pays for them less and less by the export of goods, and more and more by services, or by the income derived from her foreign investments. The trade balance is always the outstanding factor in the account, but its relative importance has diminished to a marked degree.

BALANCE OF INCOME AND EXPENDITURE IN THE
TRANSACTIONS (OTHER THAN THE LENDING
AND REPAYMENT OF CAPITAL) BETWEEN THE
UNITED KINGDOM AND ALL OTHER COUNTRIES

(Drawn up by the Board of Trade)

(Millions of pounds)

	1925	1926	1927	1928	1929
Excess of Imports of Merchandise [1]	395	477	392	358	366
Invisible Exports:					
Estimated net national shipping income	124	120	140	130	130
Estimated net income from overseas investments	250	270	270	285	285
Estimated net receipts from short interest, commissions, etc.	75	75	78	95	102
Total	449	465	488	510	517
Estimated total credit balance on items specified above	+54	—12	+96	+152	+151

[1] There are certain unimportant differences between these figures and those given by the Board of Trade, as the latter include the import and export of precious metals.

The striking feature is that the profits of the
country are now produced less by industry and exports, and more by the merchant marine, commerce,

finance, and foreign investments, or, to use the time-honoured expression, by the "invisible exports." With an export trade equal to only seven-tenths of the imports, the old dictum that England pays for her foreign purchases by the sale of manufactured goods abroad, no longer holds good, for in that case three-tenths would not be paid for. Thus we cannot conclude that the country is losing its wealth; indeed, the contrary could be argued. Possibly part of it may be leaking out in other ways, but in the last analysis a definite state of equilibrium exists, though the basis is somewhat altered. This explains the paradox that for the past ten years England has been able to support, almost with ease, a sterile amorphous mass of over a million unemployed.

Whether this evolution is healthy or not, is quite another matter; the essential point is that the nation has to readjust herself to new world conditions in which she no longer retains her old favoured position as an exporter. Such is the trend of the penetrating comments on this subject made by a speaker at the Royal Statistical Society;[1] "The 'invisible' people

[1] Dr. E. C. Snow, *Some Observations on Trade Forecasting and Prices.* Memorandum read before the Royal Statistical Society, June, 1926.

are getting the business. We may feel that it would be better for twelve men to be engaged in making boots for export rather than that one insurance broker should be making commissions of £5000 per year on foreign business; but the fact remains that those from whom we buy prefer the invisible to the visible method of payment for their food and raw materials, and we shall have to recognize the fact."

If we turn back to the table drawn up by the Board of Trade, on page 125, we easily confirm the truth of these telling observations. At first sight the deficit in the trade balance looks rather alarming, but we must not be over-impressed. The British economic framework is supple and many-sided, embracing all manner of revenues that originate neither on her own soil, nor from commercial activity carried on at home. "Rome is no longer in Rome," might well be said of this England, over-developed to the extreme, and with her centre of gravity virtually beyond her own frontiers. The 130 millions earned by the merchant marine, the 65 millions from commissions and brokerage, are evidence of commercial and financial activity, but not of industrial. The 285 millions derived from foreign investments also are financial and colonial, or even *rentier* in character, and again not industrial. It would be better if more merchandise were exported and more workmen employed, for then the country would be healthier socially. However, such as she is, England has managed to survive without catastrophe possibly the most difficult and critical years in her history.

We thus witness a regrouping of remunerative activity, for different sources of wealth are being tapped today to supply the national revenue; and moreover, there is a new distribution of the purchasing power amongst the various classes of society. On the one hand, at the moment when many manufacturing firms are losing money, the substantial profits acquired from commerce, finance, and foreign investment, are making their presence felt in the home market, by helping to maintain the level of consumption. In addition—and this is even more important—the social policy of the country, being decidedly democratic, has provided the masses with abundant funds, and in so doing has converted them into increasingly interesting customers.

Many millions of pounds have been put into the hands of the poor by the dole, by pensions of every sort, war and otherwise, and by the lavish handing out of Poor Law relief. The unemployed and needy of days gone by never dreamed of laying their hands on so much wealth. This change in the distribution of the national revenue has had much the same effect on consumption as might have resulted from a real increase in national wealth, especially as this relief money is never saved, but is thrown at once into circulation by people who immediately gratify their needs and desires. The home market thus created among the masses, is capable of supporting new industries at the very moment when the export trade, the traditional basis of British prosperity, is declining. In spite of prolonged depressions and of tremendous unemployment, the volume of purchases made by the people has not diminished; it has even increased, according to the Colwyn Committee.[1]

This improvement in the standard of living of the masses has been obtained, not by any genuine increase in national wealth, but by a fresh distribution of the national income. High wages, economically unjustified, have resulted in reduced profits for capital, while the social services have been paid for by taxes weighing heavily on production and in-

[1] Report of the Committee on National Debt and Taxation (Colwyn Report), 1927.

herited fortunes. Wealth is thus being redistributed on new lines, the country having decided to favour the masses at the expense of the minority. The old wealthy classes and also the *rentier* class have suffered most by this fiscal policy, yet they strive to maintain their former standards, which can only be done at the expense of savings—another conclusion arrived at by the Colwyn Committee. Since the working-class has improved its lot materially, although the national revenue has not increased, it follows that there has been a reduction in the real income of the other classes; but as the latter also appear to have maintained their standard of living, there must necessarily be a decrease in the total saving power of the nation.

Here we have a striking contrast between the post-War attitude of the two allies, England and France. In England the producer has been fleeced in order to pay the *rentier* and to maintain the workman. But the *rentier* has not profited, because a considerable part of his coupon has been taken back in taxes. This money has been distributed to the workmen in the form of social services, and has gone straight up in smoke. In France, on the contrary, the *rentier* has been squeezed to stake the producer, who

has used the money to re-equip his factories. Thus
the one dissipates in current expenses potential savings which otherwise would have gone eventually
into production, while the other pilfers the savings
of generations in order to transform them into pro-
ductive capital. Two opposite policies: which is
right? For a Biblical comparison, always most ap-
propriate when discussing England, one turns to the
parable of the Wise and the Foolish Virgins. . . .
But how astonishing to find that it is the French
who are wise!

3. THE FOREIGN INVESTMENT POLICY

This survey of the British position does not
necessarily contradict the findings of the Board of
Trade, whose optimism, however, does seem rather
paradoxical. In spite of so much comfort, leisure,
and amusements, England does not appear to be
in a healthy state; moreover, the optimism of the
Board of Trade is only relative, for although the
country undoubtedly does show a credit balance,
this balance is now so reduced that she has considerably less capital available for investment
abroad. She is still making money, but as she insists
on a certain standard of living, her savings may not

be enough to maintain her nineteenth-century rôle of silent partner to the rest of the world.

This delicate point in the British economy is the key to the whole structure. England is trying to compete in international markets, and at the same time provide her people with a wage level and a standard of living which does not permit costs to be low enough either to export profitably, or to attract the capital necessary for the development and upkeep of her manufacturing. Instead of freeing industry from its chains, the Government piles on more every day in its eagerness to compensate the workmen for the discomforts of the situation, by paying them for their unemployment, almost for their leisure, at the expense of the community at large. The beneficiary regards the dole as quite natural, and when he is consulted, refuses to give up a system so much to his liking. The day of reckoning is simply postponed, for the State is carrying on only by requisitioning or sequestrating on one pretext or another the capital accumulated by earlier generations, which should not be used for current expenses. Once this reserve is exhausted—or hidden away to escape requisition—England risks finding herself on the brink of a precipice.

According to the terms used by the Board of
Trade, the surplus in the balance sheet represents
the sum available for foreign investments. If there
were no credit balance, England could not go in for
this type of investment, and if the surplus were
very limited, the possibility of carrying on such a
financial policy would be proportionately reduced.
Now England has never considered her foreign investments merely as an excess of national wealth
overflowing her borders, the use of which at home
could conveniently be dispensed with. On the contrary, she regards it as an essential part of her
make-up, destined to bring in a crop of new and
profitable customers. Loans made to the Argentine
or Brazil always signify a potential order for rails
or locomotives—the receipt of the order is merely
postponed. British economists can hardly conceive
of England the exporter, without the corollary of
England the international lender of capital. This
was the system on which she lived and flourished
in the nineteenth century, for in those days the City,
with the possible exception of France, was the only
international sleeping partner of any account, and
British industry alone could furnish new countries with the equipment they required. There were

two aspects to the same operation, the foreign investment was the preliminary to an eventual sale of exports, but the investment was only made possible thanks to the profits on exports.

We can appreciate the anxiety with which the well-informed Englishman watches any reduction in the surplus of capital available for foreign investments. If the United States definitely captures the position of sleeping partner and world financier, it will sooner or later capture the markets which have hitherto been under British influence. The Americans are extensively purchasing control of various enterprises throughout the world, and this inevitably puts orders in the way of their industry, and provides employment for American personnel. Canada, though part of the Empire, and the Argentine, though British in sympathy and suspicious of American activity, are two striking examples of this tendency of markets changing hands.

A comparison between the total loans issued on the London market in 1913 and 1928, clearly proves that although England is still able to invest abroad, she can do so on the same scale as before, only at the risk of a severe hemorrhage of her resources.

ISSUES MADE ON THE LONDON MARKET [1]

(Millions of pounds)

	1913	1928
English	35 (18%)	264 (74%)
Colonial and Foreign	161 (82%)	105 (26%)
Total issues	196	369

[1] The year 1928 has been chosen as being more nearly normal than the following years.

This table proves that, taking into account the reduced purchasing power of the pound sterling, the total volume of issues is even greater than before the War, but the ultimate destination of the capital subscribed is entirely different. On the one hand the proportion of issues for the home market has risen, by a complete reversal from 18 per cent. in 1913 to 74 per cent. in 1928, while, on the other hand, foreign loans have been correspondingly reduced from 82 per cent. to 26 per cent. Further, if we consider the total amount of the foreign and colonial loans, we find a still more striking decrease, denoting a great change in the character of the London market, a change which warrants careful study.

If we are to believe the Board of Trade figures, England still overflows financially, thanks to her credit balance, but the margin is narrower than in the past. Before the War, according to generally accepted estimates, her credit balance exceeded 200 millions, but now, in a relatively good year like 1928, it is only about 150 millions. A new feature enters in, however, namely that in proportion to the total issues, England now requires a far larger share for herself. The reason is not far to seek. Formerly, her great basic industries lived, flourished, and expanded on their own resources. Thanks to their steady profits they had plenty of capital, and did not need to come to London to borrow it. Today, after a long period of depression during which textiles, coal, iron, and steel, etc., have lost money almost every year, the basic industries have been forced to turn for aid to those whose profession it is to lend money. The reorganization of an entire branch of the cotton industry under the direction—almost under the pressure—of the City, is an unheard-of event which speaks volumes regarding the decline of Manchester. The position of London as the financial capital of the nation has thus been accentuated, but it has meant a loss of international elasticity. Not that London has ceased to occupy an important rôle as an international lender—twenty re-

cent foreign loans are there to prove the contrary
—but international borrowers are gradually discovering that there are other doors at which to
knock.

One feels at once that the latent danger of this
situation is that there might not be sufficient capital
available to support continually this extensive policy
of foreign loans. Should the day arrive when the
excess of imports over exports is no longer counter-
balanced by invisible exports, then England would
have to abandon her century-old policy of foreign
investments. This would indirectly but surely endanger her future exports, and internationally
would be taken as an unmistakable sign of decline.

Under these circumstances a revival of thrift is
considered vital to the welfare of the nation, for in
the absence of a general increase in wealth, it is only
by voluntary self-denial on the part of every one
that sufficient reserves can be built up to maintain
England's position as the world's capitalist. True,
the English still save, and save large amounts; according to the Colwyn Report, the national savings
in 1925 were about 450 to 500 millions, as compared
with 350 to 400 millions before the War. This appears to be progress, but in reality it covers up a

decline, for we must consider the lower purchasing value of the pound sterling. As there has been no reduction in the capital available for the home-market, it is the foreign investments which have suffered. To recover her former prestige, the country must either earn more or spend less, and the second alternative she does not seem willing to accept, not for the moment, at any rate.

It may be that by her taxation and extravagant social services she is hindering the formation of new capital, and even squandering what she already has. The purchasing power of the masses allows them to spend freely, and taking into account the increase in population, has even given rise to swollen imports. This purchasing power is to a great extent provided by moneys distributed by the Budget, which pass into the hands of the people to go almost entirely into current expenditure with little hope of being saved. Mark you, the wealth so consumed is to a great extent provided by taxes levied not only on income but also on capital, for every year, under the deceptive heading of Death Duties, the Government makes a genuine capital levy and dissipates the proceeds largely in unproductive expenditures. Moreover, the sliding scale of taxation has been

constantly altered, until it now weighs mercilessly
on large fortunes. Two-thirds of the Budget is
borne today by direct taxation, although before the
War the proportion was only one-half. The large
tax-payer is thankful if he can avoid breaking
into his capital, but it is difficult for him to lay anything aside. Money is thus taken from the classes
who could save it, and is given to those who consume
it thoughtlessly; it is like a running sore that is
draining wealth away from those who could use it
productively.

Instead of being kept for the creation of new
enterprises, for the rationalization of old industries,
or for the building up of foreign loans which would
eventually bring profitable exports, the money so
extorted is spent on better food, more comfortable
houses, leisure, sport, and travel. The country lives
better, but it is weakening its reserves against the
future. It may not be impoverished, but it has reduced its margin of safety.

Nor is this the only danger, for quite apart from
the custom of investing abroad which has been
facilitated by Britain's unrivalled banking system,
other factors are driving her capital out of the
country. Although the nation may not be able to

afford it, the tendency is to make foreign investments in excess of the balance available, as it is
hardly tempting to put money into British companies
which are on the decline, and which during the past
ten years have paid only insignificant dividends, or
in many cases nothing at all. Even in businesses that
are not being ruined, the net profit, after wages and
social services have been met, is not sufficient to
make investment attractive. So capital is deserting
them, and turning naturally to countries where the
yield is greater.

Under present circumstances it is less expensive
for an Englishman with a fixed income to live in
France than at home—hence the well-known exodus
to the French watering-places on the Channel or
the Riviera. As capital reasons in exactly the same
way, there is a danger of a similar exodus, which
at times becomes a veritable flight. The English
taxpayer has always been considered a model of
virtue; indeed, his fiscal patriotism is unique, for he
has paid his taxes for generations, not only punctu-
ally, but ungrudgingly. In England one finds little
of that instinct for fiscal fraud which is so widespread in France; but a policy of taxation that is
manifestly excessive has now tried the Englishman

to the utmost. I do not wish to insinuate that he is not still strictly honest, but occasionally he seems to have lost his conscientiousness in the matter of paying taxes. For example, he will devise methods of investing his capital so as to avoid taxation, and if he is rich he is especially anxious to protect it from the risk of sure destruction. If he happens to be a Conservative and the government in power is Labour there is possibly a certain political craftiness in his attitude. For under the MacDonald Cabinet of 1924, and still more so in 1930, the country experienced a genuine flight of capital.

At times like the present, when capital is entirely fluid, such movements respond instantly to the slightest fears of the investing public, and also to the appeal of better terms offered by the foreigner. There are ten thousand ways in which this hemorrhage takes place, and it is difficult either to prevent it or even measure it. The country is thus tempted to invest abroad more than is justified, and at the same time it no longer attracts short-term money seeking a good yield. The unmistakable signs of this disorder are the latent weakness in the pound which comes to light periodically, and the persistence with which gold leaves the country. These tendencies can be combated only by a policy of dear money, the standard method of applying a brake to the export of capital. This puts the country in a dilemma, for to protect the pound necessitates a high discount rate, and this, in turn, injures industry. Here again we are faced with contradictions in the fundamental requirements of the country—a fatal characteristic of post-War Britain.

The London market is experiencing so much difficulty in retaining its gold that one wonders whether the balance of payments is really quite as reassuring as the Board of Trade makes out. No doubt the entries in the accounts are accurate enough, but the movement of capital has been deliberately omitted. One receives a general impression of insecurity: gold leaves the country because imports are greater than exports, because expenses are greater than receipts, because more money is invested abroad than is received from abroad, because more sterling is offered than is bid for.

France, on the other hand, can and actually does purchase gold in spite of her unfavourable trade balance, because she hoards, or, in other words, does not spend all she earns. This is very simple reasoning, but the British public refuses to accept it. When the franc was depreciating from 1923 to 1926, the French cried out indignantly at each new drop: "It is England's fault!" The British Press, with the condescension of an elder sister, laughed at their monetary simplicity, and not without reason. But read the same British Press in 1930, and you will find that it, in turn, says that the monetary nationalism of France is intolerable, and is the real cause of all the trouble! London, in her time of stress, is no more reasonable than Paris.

Whatever may be the cause of this gold crisis—the term is no exaggeration—it indicates a weakened monetary position, and also the serious fact that the international trade routes have begun to avoid British ports instead of bringing to them the financial tributes of the world. The optimism with which so many of the English buoy up their spirits is not entirely justified, although it is difficult to tell whether we are dealing with a passing phrase, due to the post-War confusion throughout the world, or whether the change is destined to endure.

Some men, when they reach maturity, lose, during the next few years, several pounds in weight. They live in perfect health with a body slightly reduced in size, and the rest of their organism accommodates itself spontaneously to the change. If this is the case with England, she obviously must adapt herself, and already one can perceive signs pointing in this direction.

CHAPTER V

SPONTANEOUS REACTIONS

I. POPULATION

IT IS difficult to say whether the trouble is too little work or too many Englishmen; unemployment or over-population.

This sounds like the subject of an academic debate, but the fact remains that for the past ten years there has been a surplus of a million men, and no one knows what to do with them. It is not generally realized that in the seventeenth century England contained only about 5½ million people, and in 1815 the whole of the United Kingdom had hardly more than 15 millions. In 1921, however, Great Britain alone had a population of 42,766,000, and today this figure has probably increased to more than 45 millions. Thus the population had more than trebled within a century, the rise being continuous even during the decade of the Great War, although in that period the rate of increase was slower. In 1921, in spite of losses by the War and emigration, England and Wales contained 1,875,000 more people than in 1911. The persistence of unemployment evidently proves that under present conditions the organism is unable to absorb this new surplus.

Even in the nineteenth century, England felt the latent menace of saturation, but eluded it partly by prosperity, partly by emigration, which on the eve of the War amounted to about 400,000 people annually. After the Armistice the Government tried to re-establish this healthy export of population which had been suspended during hostilities, but it has fallen permanently to a level which is insufficient to relieve the high blood pressure. In 1925 emigration amounted to 140,594, and in 1928 to only 136,834.

One of the reasons for this decrease in comparison with 1914 is the change in the attitude of the countries that previously received European immigrants. They do not want any more, or at any rate will now accept only settlers who are prepared to go on the land, while they put a thousand obstacles in the way of industrial labourers. Since the immigration laws of 1920 and 1924, the entrance into the United States has been almost hermetically sealed, and even within the Empire itself, the Dominions, in spite of their fine speeches, welcome the human exports of the Mother Country with little better grace. It is an undeniable fact that the policy of assisted migration to the Dominions has failed, for although it has accomplished something, the results are little more than mediocre, and since the beginning of the world-depression they have been extremely poor. As soon as unemployment appears in Australia or Canada, there is no gainsaying the arguments of those who demand that the doors should be shut.

Another difficulty, and this being a symptom is even more serious, is that the English no longer wish to emigrate as they used to in the nineteenth century. Then the cream of the population, the most ambitious and energetic, ventured forth overseas, for they lost patience with an environment that was already overcrowded. This same fine type still exists, and it is these men that the emigration authorities select and try to entice overseas, though possibly it would be better for the Mother Country if they stayed at home. The masses, however, are becoming more and more amorphous and lacking in initiative. They simply remain where they are, especially the unemployed, who never dream of emigrating, for by nature the good-for-nothing and the weaklings do not react against adversity, but wait passively for something to turn up.

Today they put up even less of a fight, since a demagogue Government supports them in idleness. Why should they make the slightest effort? If they lose their jobs, the dole will give them almost as much as their wages. Even if the industries which provided their livelihood are closed down for good, why should they and their families move away in search of a new home, when the Government is willing to maintain them, emplanted around the skeleton of the abandoned mine or factory? The evils of this short-sighted policy, which we have already discussed, are important in this connection, for they prevent a natural reaction which, though painful, might save the situation in the end. No Frenchman can reproach any one for being fond of his countryside and his own way of living, or for declining to be pulled up by the roots, and yet such passivity is obviously retarding any solution of the problem.

If this surplus of the new generation can be induced neither to leave nor to work profitably at home, we are forced to the conclusion that it would

be better if they had never been born. This seems
to be the reply of nature herself. Up to 1881-85 the
survival rate in England was high, for in spite of
a fairly serious death-rate the birth-rate was even
greater. In the period of 1881-85, for example, the
birth-rate reached 35.5 per thousand, but with the
death-rate at 19.4 the very considerable margin of
16.1 per thousand was left. From then on, up to
the War, this survival rate was maintained, for the
decline in the birth-rate was offset by a similar decline in the death-rate. Today, however, the death-
rate has reached a level from which it can scarcely
be reduced, whereas the birth-rate continues to go
down. By March 1930 the birth-rate had fallen to
16.2 per thousand, although it was still 23.6 in the
period of 1911-15. At the same time, the death-rate
decreased from 14.3 to only 13.5. Under these conditions the survival rate dropped rapidly to 9.3 per
thousand on the eve of the War, and to 4.5 in 1919,
and the present figure is as low as 2.3.

Recognized experts estimate that the population
of Great Britain will continue to grow until the
decade of 1941-51, when it will reach 48 or 49 millions, and stabilize itself at that level; the curve will
then be analogous to that of France. Already the

British birth-rate of 16.2 per thousand is lower than the French rate; in fact, it is one of the lowest in Europe. England, the country of Malthus, has encouraged birth-control propaganda since about 1880, with no contrary influences at work. As the country is over-populated and non-Catholic, the sentimental attitude towards this subject is very different from ours in France. Large families are not considered a duty—rather the reverse—and since the unemployment crisis they have been openly discredited. An upperclass Englishman once actually apologized to me for having as many as three children, but a French Catholic bourgeois would have apologized for not having more than three. The points of view are diametrically opposed. One can say that contraception is almost officially encouraged, and the Anglican Church itself, though hostile at first, no longer dares forbid it entirely.

Owing to the menace of congestion, the British people have, consciously or unconsciously, been influenced by the most pressing aspect of the situation. While in France we worry about the steady depletion of our conscript classes, the English note with satisfaction any reduction in the numbers of their working-class population that has to be absorbed annually into industry. They are relieved to learn that the number of young people reaching the age of fourteen or fifteen has fallen from 1,641,000 in 1921 to 1,600,000 in 1928, and should drop to 1,381,000 in 1931, and only 1,384,000 in 1940.[1] No one seems to fret about this reduction in population, though possibly the future may bring a change in sentiment. For the moment the English see only the immediate needs of the situation, and look on the decline as a potential reduction in the unemployed.

This movement towards a lower birth-rate dates back to the third quarter of the last century, which reminds us that we must turn back to that period to find the underlying causes of the present crisis. Without a doubt, this reduction is a natural movement, the spontaneous reaction of an organism instinctively seeking a state of equilibrium, by whatever means are available. Nevertheless, the country is defeating its own efforts, as we have now shown at least ten times, by its very policy of social services which distort all normal relationships. The restriction of the birth-rate is less marked amongst

[1] Figures published by the Committee on Industry and Trade.

the lower classes than among the better educated,
and when the sense of responsibility of the masses
has been impaired by the certainty of regular public assistance, it is almost negligible. Just as the
inveterate unemployed refuses to emigrate, so he
also neglects to limit the number of his children.
He has nothing else to do but procreate, and he
counts on the community to take care of his offspring.

What a curious contrast between recklessness of
governments on the one hand, and the canniness of
nature on the other! Though the community is extravagant financially, it is trying involuntarily to
adapt itself to the requirements of an age in which
thrift should be the keynote.

2. THE INDUSTRIAL CENTRE OF GRAVITY

A phenomenon which is often discussed and to
which we have already drawn attention, is that unemployment has affected various branches of industry in proportion to the degree that they are dependent on exports and based on coal. Some of the
hardest hit areas are already losing their population—for example, many parts of South Wales,
where the coal mines have been closed without hope

of ever being reopened. At first the people cling to the village, rooted there by the dole which allows them to hold on for a while. The time will come—or should come—sooner or later, when they will have to move on. The day of reckoning is inevitable, and it is beyond the power of man to postpone it indefinitely. The policy of the Industrial Transference Board aims at assisting geographic redistribution by stimulating or aiding the migration of individuals.

Here again, nature has not awaited the action of governments, but has worked alone in her own way to achieve the same end. One can already perceive a spontaneous movement of population from the north of England towards the south, from the mining areas towards London and the Thames valley. This tentative migration may be considered as the first visible after-effect of the attack on the coal monopoly. In the nineteenth century the centre of gravity of the British economic structure was irresistibly attracted towards the coal basins of the north; the twentieth century may produce a new equilibrium, less strictly dependent on the Black Country.

About 1926 the Ministry of Labour worked out

statistics showing the geographic distribution of unemployment. These tables disclosed the first symptoms of this evolution, and all subsequent evidence has confirmed their findings. The destinies of the north and the south seem to be diverging. The two zones can be divided approximately by a line starting from the Severn, passing through Stratford and the High Peak, and ending in Scarborough; the southern zone seems to be gaining at the expense of the northern.[1]

In 1923, 54.3 per cent. of the population insured against unemployment, *i.e.* the industrial man-power, was to be found in the north-eastern zone, as against 45.7 per cent. in the southern; but in 1929 the north had declined to 52 per cent. while the south rose to 48 per cent. This is only an indication as yet, but the trend is definite. The movement may possibly continue to increase, for among the insured population of the north are many unemployed who will inevitably have to emigrate to the south sooner or later. For example, a large proportion of the coal-mining population will eventually be superfluous, and these people will have to seek work elsewhere, and as they will probably find it in the south, we

1 *Ministry of Labour Gazette*, November 1929.

may assume that the majority of British workmen will be located there in the near future. The region around London and the area south-east of the line from Portsmouth to the Wash, which we shall call the south-east, even in 1929 contained 26 per cent. of the insured population, as compared with 24.2 per cent. in 1923. South Wales, on the contrary, is definitely declining, not merely relatively but actually, for it is losing its population.

The geographic distribution of unemployment emphasizes this contrast still more clearly. As we saw on page 48, and on the maps on pp. 46 and 47, in the year 1928, before the world-depression began, unemployment was already serious in the north, was mild in the bordering zone, and was insignificant in the Thames valley and throughout the south-east generally, where from 1927 to 1929 there was even a mild boom. Its industries being less specialized, Birmingham suffered less than Manchester, while Coventry, Bristol, London, and the small industrial towns located round London, experienced real prosperity.

In our pessimism over the slump of 1930, we must not overlook the fact that, although the north declined after the General Strike of 1926, life re-

turned with renewed vigour in the older districts
of the south, whence it had departed about a century ago. England's centre of gravity still remains
in the Black Country, but it has started to move,
and is now being attracted steadily towards London
and the Midlands. The old mines of the Tyne, of
Scotland, and of Wales, are being deserted in
favour of the Midland pits and those in Kent. At
the same time, while the industries of Lancashire,
Yorkshire, and Northumberland have been uniformly depressed since 1921, those of the south,
comparatively new in many cases, have been quite
successful.

Iron and steel, coal, cottons and woollens, have
been struggling against hopeless adversity. Yet furniture and the building trades, motor cars, artificial
silk, electrical equipment, not to mention the theatre,
cinema, breweries, distilleries, and hotels, have all
given proof of remarkable development. Even in
1926, the year of the General Strike, these industries blossomed out, paradoxical as it may seem.
In their 1927 reports, the labour inspectors speak
with satisfaction of "the region about London, which
was developing in a most remarkable manner." They
drew attention to "the astonishing prosperity of

Coventry." The Morris motor works have turned Oxford into a manufacturing city, and the intellectuals, in the exquisite and cultural environment of their colleges, shudder at the thought that in fifteen years' time the old university town may be a second Birmingham.

The reasons for the irresistible gravitation from the north towards the south must probably be sought outside the relatively narrow industrial framework that we have studied so far. As a matter of fact the extreme north of Scotland and especially the Hebrides, have for some time been losing their population, for the simple reason that no one wishes to live in such a rugged climate or so far away from the world. The Lowlands, which formerly attracted an invasion of Irish, have no longer the same place in the British economic system. This identical situation is to be found in the gloomy Black Country of Lancashire, Yorkshire, and Northumberland, where the energy and Puritanism of the nineteenth century had its industrial headquarters.

London, and the London area, are now taking the lead, for London is the capital city in every sense of the word, even more than Paris is to France. Everything begins and ends in London. It faithfully reflects every point of view in the nation as a whole. The management of Big Business, whether commercial or industrial, is gradually locating its headquarters there, and it is there that both capital and brains are to be found. Ambitious young men are afraid to accept positions elsewhere, for they cannot afford to be far from the real centre of power. If Cobden could return to his country today, it is doubtful whether he would choose Manchester as the seat of his activities.

It is hard to say whether this attraction towards the south is entirely a national affair, or whether it is the effect of the change in the international currents outside of England herself. For the last fifty years the main traffic between North America and Europe followed the line of New York-Liverpool with a branch line to Glasgow, but since the beginning of the century there has been a certain movement in favour of the line New York-Plymouth-Southampton, or possibly New York-Plymouth-Cherbourg-Le Havre-Paris. To prove this, one need only note how much the great shipping companies have altered their ports of call and European termini during the past few years.

Now that a direct and close relationship has been

established between the United States and the European continent instead of going via England as hitherto, the English Channel has become the axis and the Irish Sea has been pushed to the edge of the picture. A significant indication of this change is obtained by comparing the proportion of the total number of passengers to Europe who used to go through Liverpool fifty years ago, with the proportion going through today. England, considered as a whole, does not thus occupy the same position in relation to the Continent as she did before. The Channel is now the main traffic route between North America and Europe, and this is possibly one reason why the activity, which for a century had abandoned these regions for the Black Country of the North, has now returned to the green pastures of the south.

3. VARIATIONS IN INDUSTRIAL PROFITS

The comparative yields of various industries give a new explanation of this contrast. Leaving to one side the acute and widespread depression of 1930, we find in the following table the way in which different branches of production made profits in the years 1926 to 1929.

PROFITS ON CAPITAL IN VARIOUS INDUSTRIES [1]

(1926-1929)

	1926	1927	1928	1929
Very Prosperous:				
Oil and Petroleum	20.7%	17.4%	11.3%	11.7%
Rubber Plantations	35.0	22.7	8.5	7.9
Tobacco	19.4	19.7	19.2	18.7
Breweries	15.7	15.3	16.6	15.6
Tea	42.1	34.8	30.5	27.4
Less Prosperous:				
Motor Industry	10.9	14.2	7.1	21.7
Cycle Industry	13.7	12.7	10.7	12.6
Shipping	13.1	10.1	9.6	9.3
General Stores	10.6	11.9	12.5	13.6
Slightly Prosperous:				
Engineering	5.8	5.3	7.1	8.4
Cottons	6.5	8.5	11.4	10.7 [2]
In a very Serious Condition:				
Coal, Iron, and Steel ....—1.5		—.4	.8	1.3 [3]

[1] Profits remaining after the payment of general expenses, interest on debentures and amortization of equipment.

[2] The group of textiles drawn up by *The Times* includes one company that was exceptionally prosperous, *i.e.* J. & P. Coats & Company, Ltd. The average figure gives a result that is apparently optimistic, though the industry as a whole is seriously injured.

[3] Deficit.

Little comment is needed, for this table shows the astonishing diversity in the fortunes of British business since the War. On the black list we have coal and iron, once the country's pride and the basis of her power. Their statements of earnings show a deficit, for since 1925 the coal industry in general has been losing money, and the heavy metals have been little better off, especially as both felt the full effect of the General Strike. For example, in 1927, an exceptionally bad year for the whole country, eighteen typical metallurgical companies, chosen by *The Times,* representing an invested capital of about 70 million pounds, lost 2½ millions, no fewer than thirteen suffering heavily. In 1929, out of twelve mining and metallurgical companies, chosen by *The Times,* the profit was only £411,000 on an invested capital of 32 millions, but in 1927 there was a loss of £139,000, and in 1926 of £545,000. Obviously, such conditions can lead only to ruin, for with profits of 2 per cent. or 3 per cent.—even if that were assured—it is absolutely impossible to pay dividends, build up reserves, replace materials, and attract new capital to maintain and develop production.

Nevertheless a second and entirely different category of enterprises did succeed during the period under consideration. The breweries, distilleries, and departmental stores, being closely linked with the consuming power of the masses, have benefited indirectly from the extravagant distribution of the social services; but others, such as motor cars, bicycles, electrical equipment, furniture, artificial silk, and gramophones were similarly affected, although they cater to a better *clientèle*. These twentieth-century industries, which were more or less neglected in England before the War, are experiencing a sort of rebirth, especially in the south and the region bordering on the Black Country, and it is comforting to find that English technique in these lines is absolutely first class.

The last category is perhaps the most significant. It contains various colonial enterprises, which though they may be profitless for several years and astonishingly sensitive to international depressions, will nevertheless, at other times yield fabulous returns. When world trade is good, as it was from 1925 to 1929, the British investor draws an enormous revenue from tea, tobacco, oil, and rubber, and this explains why British capital is attracted abroad in preference to England. This confirms our earlier observation, that under present world conditions, the British Isles are no longer the "chosen land" where capital yields the best results. The country has reached the point of diminishing returns, after which it is advisable, according to Ricardo's law, to go further afield.

If we examine the geographic location of these various enterprises, we are interested to note that the prosperous ones are mainly established in the south or on the borders of the Black Country. Comparing 1929 with 1923, we find that seventy-one industries were making progress, in so far as the number of employees was concerned.[1] These included silk, cement, heating apparatus, scientific and musical instruments, electric cables, paints and varnishes, bricks, electric appliances, furnishings, hotels, motor cars, rubber, paper, cocoa, tobacco, breweries, chemicals, and retail distribution. In the majority of these seventy-one industries, most of the personnel was drawn from the district south-east of the Severn-Scarborough line. On the other hand, twenty-nine industries were losing ground: ship-building, heavy metals, engineering, woollens, cottons, docks, etc., all of which are concentrated in Lancashire, Yorkshire, Northumberland-Durham, Scotland, and Wales.

Let us carry the analysis a step further. It is the heavy industries—those dependent on coal, and

[1] *Ministry of Labour Gazette,* November 1929.

working primarily for export—that are declining, while the successful ones are those in which raw material is unimportant in comparison with the value of the finished article. The latter work mainly, though not entirely, for the home market, which explains why they are situated in the south rather than the north. In the first place, not being strictly dependent on coal, they are not obliged to be close to the pit-head, especially as power transmission has so greatly improved; also many of them have been electrified. The south suits them better, as the climate is preferable, the atmosphere clearer, and the ground rents lower, since factories can now be set up almost anywhere. Also they are rather glad to establish themselves well away from the districts where the trade unions are so influential and well organized that they have become too tyrannical. Finally, since they are aiming at a national *clientèle*, they need not be located on the sea-board, as in the case of the exporting industries. Again, proximity to the capital, that enormous centre of distribution, can quite legitimately be considered of extreme importance. Accordingly, many small towns in the south, which once were noted for their manufactures and then were deserted for over a hundred

years, have been reawakened from their slumber by
the return of new and unexpected activity.

4. A NEW EQUILIBRIUM

This new division of economic vitality can be regarded as an instinctive effort towards industrial
recovery. Every individual clings to existence, and
an organism, whether a society or an individual,
lives as best it can. In this respect the British organism has anticipated the insight of the observers, and
the initiative of the rulers. Now that her exporting
industries have grown old and battered, and can
give but indifferent support, England, in order to
live, turns towards her still prosperous commerce,
her still influential international finance, and her
foreign and colonial investments which still constitute a reserve of inestimable importance. She
even turns to those new industrial activities, which
in the home market are profiting by the rate of
national expenditure. By such means, and also
thanks to her great reserves of wealth, she has undoubtedly created a certain equilibrium.

Yet in so doing England is changing. As a result of a movement which started years ago, she is
inclined to place her hopes in her rôle of world

broker, in the management of her great interests abroad, or in the creation and protection of a home market the value of which she is at last beginning to appreciate. One cannot say that industrial exports are no longer her first preoccupation, but they certainly do not claim the same predominance as formerly. England reminds one of those great industrial families, powerful and old, whose factories have declined in importance, but whose immense accumulated wealth has been put into other safe investments. They must not be judged by the tools which they used in the beginning, for these are no longer the essential factors in their fortunes or their power.

England is able to carry on in this way, and even prosper, although her exporting industries have now been outclassed. Her wealth is not entirely contained in the vast equipment concentrated in Birmingham, Manchester, Leeds, or Glasgow, for it is finding its way more and more into the tea plantations of India, the rubber groves of Malay, and the oil wells of half a dozen countries. Above all, it is centred in the City of London, where commerce and finance are closely interwoven, and the outlook embraces the entire world. Huge sums earned in international transactions, often remote from British soil, eventually return to the old country. Just as high wages and lavish public assistance have stimulated industry, so these foreign profits have also helped to build up a new type of production. It may be parasitical rather than nourishing, but for this very reason it is not forced to seek its customers in all four corners of the world. In this sense, England is less of an exporting nation than in the past, and more *rentier* in that she is living on the income from her investments. When attacked economically she takes the defensive—that was not the spirit of the nineteenth century!

PART II

THE REMEDIES

CHAPTER VI

THE ENGLISHMAN'S ATTITUDE

1. PUBLIC OPINION AND THE CRISIS

SOME years before the War, when George V was still Prince of Wales, he concluded a speech with the direct and simple phrase, "Wake up, England!" But even today England has not yet awakened.

The country is being shaken to its very foundations by an unprecedented crisis; its effects are new, and no one can foretell what the end will be; England is lost without a compass in this strange new twentieth century, to which she does not belong— yet the great mass of the people remain unperturbed. The average Englishman lives according to two or three ready-made formulae, emphasizing British superiority. Worse still, these formulae, which are reiterated in his Press and his text-books, infer that he is always right, so he accepts them without question. He has yet to learn, or rather re-learn, that success is attained only by work and merit, and is not the result of an acquired situation. Evidently, he will have to be thoroughly frightened before he will admit even to himself that the danger is serious, and that it is impossible to avoid it without grief and pain. Even when he voices such sentiments, one can never be quite sure that he really means what he says.

During both the War and its aftermath, the average Englishman was confronted with difficult problems, although the State undertook to solve them for him. His daily preoccupations are matters of immediate interest, the cost of living, the difficulty of finding a job, disputes over wages and working hours, and so forth, and most people do not look further ahead than this. They have little time to think about great international problems, or even about the development of their own Imperial outlook. The politicians have long realized that Imperialism has no appeal in an electoral campaign, and during the present period of stress, the atmosphere savours much of the "Little Englander." A certain lack of ambition is especially noticeable, a disinclination to go further afield in quest of fortune, a passive acceptance of one's lot wherever fate has willed. Many young men, rather than emigrate, are content to put up with a living which is mediocre and practically without possibilities.

True to his inveterate insularity, our Englishman remains entirely self-satisfied. His century-old pride prevents him from seeing, or at least appreciating, what is wrong with him, especially when he is enumerating his own shortcomings, for self-criticism is a very English affectation. The leading newspapers flatter him, and bolster up his own conviction that he belongs to a race apart, materially more civilized than Europe, intellectually more civilized than America, living on a superior plane, far above the common herd. So he does not reform, but quietly dozes on, with his head on the pillow of ready-made formulae which he never revises. His lethargy lulls him into a fatal state of optimism.

The Englishman not only shrinks from the effort needed to solve his problems; he will not even formulate them. His mental laziness is extraordinary. It bores him to think, and he is particularly hostile when any one raises a discussion of principles, upsetting his peace of mind. When he is forced into a corner, he contents himself with half-explanations, or some snap judgment which will give him an excuse to think no more about it. Perhaps this explains

why these people who live so leisurely in comparison with others, always give the impression of
charming repose. Their traditional calm is so sooth-
ing to the nerves that, with little effort, one could
imagine that time itself had ceased to flow. Such an
atmosphere is fatal: "Wake up, England!"

This lack of realism—this vague, indolent method
of setting aside realities—deceives the people as to
the respective merits of other nations. The chosen
few are well-informed, no doubt, but the average
Englishman stays at home in his island, and even
when he travels, he regards the Continent with all
the condescension of a colonial towards a native. He
cannot believe that Europe has been modernized,
that her hotels have proportionately more bathrooms
and running water than have his own, or that her
dangerous competition arises not merely from the
lower wages he loves alluding to, but also from a
new technique and a new spirit of emulation and
progress.

There is something comic in this injured superiority, which makes the Britisher consider unfair
the competition of rivals who work harder, and are
satisfied with less pretentious wages. Proud of his
standard of living, he is pleased to think that, shut

up in his castle, he will always be able to ignore the competition of people who are not afraid of strenuous work. Nothing is more difficult for the modern Englishman to realize than the essential connection between effort and result. He wishes to reap without having sown, to succeed without fatigue, to get something for nothing. Though earlier generations have understood and practised the manly philosophy of merit, so vigorously preached by Cobden, Englishmen today seem content to rely on tradition. "We have Abraham to our father," they seem to say, as if that could help them.

This country, which is so strong and brave in many ways, as it proved magnificently during the War, has not the courage to go sincerely to work, even in times of great depression. Sport, the favourite pastime, claims an alarming amount of the people's energy, and from the French point of view, lowers their preoccupations almost to a level of childishness. A cricket match becomes a national event which empties the offices and the workshops, monopolizes all attention, and drives care aside. "National Disaster," or "Can England be Saved?" is written in enormous characters on the newspaper bulletins. Is it the two million unemployed, or the fall in exports? Not at all, it is simply the defeat of a champion cricket team. When travelling in England one continually comes across athletic events, even in the middle of the week. Such meetings occur remarkably often, and never fail to attract attention, often drawing thousands of spectators. Have these people nothing to do, that they can take such generous holidays? I do not wish to exaggerate, but it does remind one of Byzantium, which could think of nothing but the circus games, even when the enemy was at its gates. "Vous deliberez!" cried Mirabeau, but "Vous vous amusez!" could be substituted in the present case. A false security, closely allied to apathy, acts as an anesthetic, and makes the English unwilling to renounce their life of ease; though under the circumstances, alas, it is no longer justified.

Let us get to the root of the problem. There is nothing radically wrong with this people. They are scrupulously honourable, and loyal in their engagements and attachments. They are models of patriotism, as any government can prove if it appeals to them for help. Yet something is lacking in this nation of honest citizens. They are among the most civilized in the world, and it may be that for this very reason, they lack the will to win. At the moment when they should be redoubling their efforts, when everything has to be reconstructed on a new pattern, they prefer to rest on their laurels. If I may say so again, England seems to be wanting in vitality.

2. THE RULING CLASS

The full significance of the situation does not escape those who reflect. They know full well that England cannot be inscribed amongst the victors of the War, which in thoughtful circles was considered a catastrophe. The English did not desire it, they endured it, and now they renounce it. After the Armistice, under an illusion which captivated even the most astute, they tried to bring back the past. They set themselves to the task with the same respect and lack of imagination that is shown by people who try to preserve intact the rooms of the great after their death. In the end they have realized that it was impossible, for, to quote the words of the Greek philosopher, "One cannot wash twice in the same water." The General Strike of 1926, which marked the end of this phase, left behind it a lasting state of discouragement.

The proletariat, at any rate, have every reason to

be satisfied. They are being maintained and, according to general opinion, are living better than ever before. But the former governing classes see only the spectre of ruin. When the British system was at its height, fortune, elegance, and political power were almost synonymous. The enjoyment of great wealth had accustomed the favoured few to a respect for money, and when they went abroad it was their money in turn that was respected. A generation ago it was the Englishman who travelled most comfortably and was the best served, but to-day the English aristocrat is living on his reserves, and no longer spends recklessly. On the Continent the English *clientèle* has lost its reputation for open-handedness, and it is the lavish Americans, the Argentinians, and the Egyptians, who attract attention and receive the fawning civilities. The English wealthy class, who yesterday were the lords of creation, were unprepared for this eventuality. They cannot understand it, protesting indignantly, after their fashion, against the new-comers. In their wounded pride they aggressively refer to themselves as the "new poor."

More serious still is the fact that a few of these aristocrats are losing their sense of fiscal integrity, that feeling of responsibility towards the State which was once one of their noblest attributes. Many no longer collaborate whole-heartedly, for they have become more eager to dodge taxation. Without losing our sense of proportion, we may say that a whole section of Belgravia is adopting towards the modern democratic State the surly contemptuous attitude of the Faubourg St. Germain.

One gathers the impression that many Englishmen admit that a decline in Britain's power is inevitable. France experienced the bitterness of a similar revelation at the close of the nineteenth century, when, after being humbled by the defeat of 1870, she perceived that the growing economic power of the new continents was steadily reducing her international importance. She has now recovered from that mood of discouragement, but her dreams of world power have gone for ever.

Must Britain also resign herself to gradual decline? In her case it would be more heart-breaking, for her influence is world-wide. Yet this seems to be the opinion of certain young men who are by no means the exception. "Supremacy of the seas?" they say. "How can we defend ourselves against the submarines, or compete with the wealth of

America? Why take part in a ruinous rivalry which leads nowhere? As for industrial supremacy, would it not be better to try to consolidate a lower volume of production by relying on a protected home market? Imperial supremacy? The Dominions keep insisting that they have their own lives to live, so why should they gravitate about us any longer? A 'Little England' would really be a happier solution."

This is simply an attack of defeatism, doubtless the same temporary depression from which all the Continental nations suffered, without exception, as a reaction from the War and inflation. Even a slight economic recovery, or the simple conviction that the Government can and will do something, would undoubtedly restore courage to many who are naturally confident. But is a return of confidence enough? To reconstruct on as dominating and as grand a scale as before requires ambition, and ambition seems to be lacking. Perhaps this defeatism is merely want of the courage necessary to carry out new and audacious programmes, or it may be the acceptance of *un fait accompli* by minds that have no imagination.

The friends of this great people—and there are many in France—are anxious to see more passion, even more pride in the struggle. We fully appreciate the link that binds us in Europe to Britain's destiny. I do not know an intellectual Frenchman who is not distressed to think of the present decline in British prestige. England today is making less sacrifice to retain her power than to increase the comforts of life. At a time when there is much glib talk about Imperialism, she is full of "Little Englanders." She seems to wilt. Is it too much democracy, or perhaps too much refinement? The ideal of a gentleman, the foundation of modern British civilization, seems to have contributed to this relaxation of fundamental energy. A gentleman, we must realize, never strives too much; it is not considered the thing. He does nothing too well; he leaves that to the professional and the champion. His perfect manners are acquired at the price of the stuff of which heroes are made. The English bulldog grip, though still strong in certain directions, is sometimes inclined to relax.

Elegance, however, has proportionately increased, and nowhere as in England do we find such supreme aristocratic tone, or such grace and dignity in times of stress. The very detachment with which the Englishman analyzes his ills, is to be found only in the most highly developed type of humanity. One breathes an atmosphere of culture that is almost Elizabethan. By a paradox which would have seemed ridiculous thirty years ago, in England one feels infinitely removed from the neo-bourgeois type of Frenchman, that thick-skinned social climber who knows so well how to defend himself.

Do not go to post-War England if you are in need of a tonic. It is not sufficiently invigorating. On the other hand, at the very moment when wealth, power, and culture are becoming dissociated, one finds there a refinement that is unequalled elsewhere.

3. THE TRANSFORMATION OF THE POLITICAL SYSTEM

The political stability of England has always been the admiration of the world. Throughout its entire structure, one feels the weight of order and discipline, and a dignity in strong contrast with the sloppiness of some of the Latin democracies. In any other country the General Strike of 1926 would inevitably have ended in a national disaster. The English mind is naturally constructive; it lends itself to co-operation, and is essentially loyal. These are first-rate qualities in the conduct of government, and in the nineteenth century they enabled

England to reap a rich reward, which was unequalled elsewhere.

Nevertheless, behind this imposing façade, England has been more contaminated than any other Western community by the exigencies of democracy —in this I am not exaggerating. In appearance her institutions have changed little since the Victorian era, when she was controlled and efficiently governed by her aristocracy. The monarchy still stands, solid and full of vitality, for the King and the Royal Family have not decreased in popularity—rather the contrary. The House of Lords assembles with the same old ceremonial, and though its powers were curtailed in 1911 by the Parliament Act, it retains most of its constitutional privileges. The peers individually enjoy considerable prestige, especially with the masses, who are even more deferential than the middle class. At Court the King and Queen are surrounded by the nobility as in olden times, and if, owing to his position, some Labour minister is present, he too wears court dress and is apparently delighted to be there. Recently, when a daughter was born to the Duchess of York, the Home Secretary, an ardent Socialist, respectfully awaited the happy event near by. In accordance with ancient custom, his presence was required, for the child one day might reign: "A great personage was about to be born." Not for a moment did our democrat protest against the inconvenience and trouble. Far from it. No subject could have been more respectful and more of a courtier than this representative of the common people.

What, then, has changed? Everything. In the last century the system was still genuinely hierarchic, and even when the submerged masses began to make demands, all they asked was a programme of practical achievement which was praiseworthy in its moderation. The direction of affairs still remained in the hands of the so-called ruling classes. It is significant to note that the social season coincided with the political season. The same men were found in both. Under such a *régime* one could make good finance and at the same time busy oneself usefully in the building up of a world empire.

By creating an entirely different set of circumstances, the war aroused a new spirit and awakened new desires among the people. The immense army of fighting men slowly began to realize that in England, as elsewhere, it was possible to lead a more comfortable life. While the soldiers were overseas their dependants—that is to say, the whole population—were more or less the wards of the nation, and this tended to weaken the feeling of direct responsibility on the part of the heads of families. It is not surprising, therefore, that when peace was restored, this socialization of the life of the people should have been perpetuated. The policy of the dole, although its initial germ can be traced far back into English history, developed immediately after the War. It was irresistible, and no government could have opposed it without risk of revolution.

Since the War the people have thus become much more socialistic in outlook than is generally realized, while their sense of political responsibility also has been seriously weakened. The truth is, they are simply profiting by a situation which suits them admirably. Under an aristocratic *régime* people have leisure and freedom of thought to consider production and to prepare for the future, but under a democratic *régime* they can think only of the distribution of wealth and of the immediate present. The masses in England are mainly concerned with getting possession of a greater proportion of the national wealth which they are to possess. They take no interest in increasing or preserving that wealth.

We are dealing with a country where the vast majority belong to the working class, and where public opinion reigns supreme. Although this popular will can be canalized or even diverted, and usually remains docile in the hands of its leaders, it is irresistible when aroused. The total effective of British industry consists of 3.7 per cent. of owners, 6.3 per cent. of independent workers, and 90 per cent. of wage-earners. How, under a *régime* of universal suffrage, is it possible to oppose or even modify the will of this 90 per cent.?

The peasant is the essential piece in the French democracy, and fundamentally he has the mentality of an employer. He hates useless expense, and he will not tolerate people who do not work. In this the majority of the English are on the other side of the fence, as is quite obvious whenever a Labour Government is in power. The proportion of the national expenditure that is spent on the masses is then increased, the dole is augmented, and the conditions under which it is distributed are slackened. The Conservatives and Liberals are scarcely better able to resist, for they too depend upon the masses for votes, and these same masses find it very pleasant to dip their hands into the nation's money-box, which they seem to think is inexhaustible. No politician has yet dared to risk his chance of re-election by proposing a serious revision of the dole, or by making a frontal attack on wages. The liberty of action of the State has thus been seriously compromised, and to reinstate it the social *régime* must be completely transformed. At the moment this eventuality seems hardly probable.

To a certain extent England is preyed upon by democracy. The idea of individual property is less deeply rooted in England than in France. Because of a sense of patriotism that is almost feudal and often even stronger than the selfishness of the French bourgeois, the so-called ruling classes in England are generally the first to give way. They understand the collective nature of landed and other property, and the thousand forms of financial wealth. They enjoy doing social-service work—that is their tradition and even their boast. As is well known, some of the most daring reforms have been carried out by the nobility. For example, Sir William Harcourt, a member of an old family of bluest blood, established the progressive scale of death duties in 1894, and it is these same Draconian taxes which today are rapidly destroying the inherited fortunes of the old aristocratic class.

Lack of resistance seems to be the distinctive trait of this social aristocracy. Year after year, month after month, they give way, wholesale and retail, as the French aristocrats did in the famous night of 4th August 1789. One feels that because traditionally they are accustomed to govern, they insist willy-nilly on remaining at the head of affairs, although it may be only to carry out a policy which will ruin them. In order to continue to hold the reins certain of their number agree to do whatever democracy asks of them. The façade will be preserved at any rate, since if a revolution ever takes place, it will be carried out by lords and gentlemen.

After all, this paradox corresponds with reality. If one does not look into the situation too closely, one would think that the chosen ones of birth and fortune are still reigning. No country has a ruling class better educated politically, more conscious of its own worth, and available in greater numbers for the task of government, even when that task entails sacrifices. An excellent team is always at hand, no matter what party is in power. On their side the common people adore this fiction, for though they may seem to be extraordinarily rash in their radicalism, they are not democratic in temperament. Give them the material advantages and assistance they demand, and they will be enchanted to follow the King, the princes, and the titled gentry.

In this jumble of make-believe and reality a new power is growing up, almost a new social class. In a country that used to boast that it was governed by amateurs, a bureaucracy is appearing. As the functions of the State multiply, the carrying out of the laws naturally becomes more complicated, and a technique is required such as only a professional administration can supply. The personnel increases automatically with each addition to the social legislation, and the new departments grow daily in size and influence. The Civil Service has thus expanded considerably since the War, and its value is very great. It is recruited by examination from well-educated and competent circles, indeed the civil servants often come from Eton, Oxford, or Cambridge, as well as from the new provincial universities.

Under such conditions it is not only the old governing class which furnishes the civil servants, but also the middle and lower middle classes, and this fact even more than the victories of Labour is democratizing the country. From a distance everything looks the same as before—the same morning coat, the same top hat, the same spats—but the spirit has changed. England is now a democracy in the full sense of the word, administered by ability, often inspired by the demagogue, still slightly tinged with snobbery. In this paradoxical country snobbishness is not necessarily a Conservative attribute.

In conclusion, we must emphasize the fact that among the Western democracies, which are all suffering from the same evil, namely, lack of responsibility on the part of the people, England is particularly affected. She is desperately handicapped in her efforts to reform, for, even in the present unprecedented crisis, no one dares come out boldly and tell the people, electorally at any rate, what they must do to break the deadlock: lower the standard of living and work harder. Many Englishmen realize this, and are not afraid to say so publicly, but on a political platform it is practically impossible. A candid Frenchman might just as well come before his electors advocating the abolition of universal suffrage! Politics cannot necessarily solve problems which are more profound than politics themselves. It is the whole rhythm of English life that must be changed. Such a reformation, it must be admitted, requires more than a mere change of Cabinet. It means nothing short of a form of revolution. And England will do everything in her power to prevent that. We must not lose sight of this reservation in studying in the following chapters the various remedies proposed.

CHAPTER VII

LAISSEZ-FAIRE OR INTERVENTION

I. RATIONALIZATION

IF MANUFACTURING costs are too high, the first remedy which suggests itself is to reduce them. Once this has been accomplished, one would start to export again, thus bringing the depression to an end. This solution is proposed by those who consider that industry should pull itself out of the mire by its own efforts, without any special aid from the State. One easily recognizes this as the purest of traditional Liberalism, which today is considered old-fashioned. Before having recourse to it, England will first try out every other expedient.

We have dwelt at length on the fact that the root of the evil is the spread between wages and prices, which tends to keep real wages at an unduly high level. A reduction in real wages would cause a corresponding reduction in unemployment, since it would reopen new zones of activity for the export trade. Every one is unanimous on this point, and many different methods are proposed for bringing real wages down.

Employers consider that the most effective way would be to reduce nominal wages—employers always do think this—but it is a lazy solution if not accompanied by a reorganization of the industry itself, as it places the whole sacrifice upon the working class. Such a programme has no chance of success in this form, for frontal attacks against wages are no better than were frontal attacks against the trenches during the War. All efforts would be hurled in vain against the well-organized resistance of the trade unions, veterans with half a century of experience in such warfare. In their wage level they are defending ground fought over and won by earlier generations, and it is a matter of honour not to retreat. Behind the workman's organizations stands the general public, composed mainly of wage-earners, who fear any reduction in the standard of living. In their heart of hearts they say to themselves, "Our turn next."

The doctrine of high wages had little popularity with the nineteenth-century economists, but today it is so firmly rooted that few dare attack it openly, and certainly no politician will willingly run the risk.

Difficulties seem to bristle up on every side. Whenever the employers propose a reduction, though they may prove that by lowering prices generally, the former purchasing power would still be maintained. The first response invariably is "Rationalize yourselves, and then we will see. If you are incapable of rationalization, you must sacrifice your profits."

Statistics prove that nominal wages under such conditions can be lowered only very slowly. They will be lowered eventually, however, in fact they have gone down a little already, and every day they drop still further, as they cannot withstand the irresistible pressure of facts. The workman, who never fully understands such subtle distinctions, will accept a greater reduction in real than in nominal wages, especially if it is done without his realizing it. With the aid of certain subterfuges this is not impossible.

With better factory organization it would be possible to reduce prices without touching nominal wages—this is the American solution, by the machine and by rationalization. It is a gigantic programme, and though in England they have talked a great deal about it during the past few years, they have been very slow in putting it into practice. This is easy to understand. In the first place, industries which are losing money have difficulty in finding the capital necessary to install costly new equipment. Also, it is no secret that the trade unions are instinctively hostile to technical improvements which might lead to a reduction in man-power. Their attitude towards rationalization reminds one of La Fontaine's fable, "Ce bloc enfariné ne me dit rien qui vaille." The liberal and progressive attitude of the American trade union is quite foreign to them. The introduction into Lancashire of the automatic loom is now arousing obstinate hostility, and this is typical of the workmen's attitude in other trades. The mental laziness with which we reproach the owner, is evidently neither the only nor yet the main reason why British industry is so backward technically. The owner is told to rationalize, but everything is against him.

In the end, the menace of ruin will impress itself upon the workman. The 1926 strike, with its innumerable and prolonged after-effects, taught him one thing, at any rate, and that was the meaning of mutual responsibility. In future if less appeal is made to his good humour and more to his self-interest, there may be some chance of making him understand. Such a policy was conceived and launched by the late Lord Melchett, and it was owing to his insistence and great authority that the leading elements in the Trades Union Council, in spite of their suspicions and resistance, were eventually convinced. The workman naturally refuses to carry the whole burden of the sacrifices necessary, but if he sees that the employer is bearing his own share, he may be persuaded to give his indispensable co-operation. After all, this attitude is to be found only where there is extraordinary prosperity, or the menace of ruin. British industry today comes under the latter heading.

Finally, consent must be obtained from the various interests which are to be grouped together. As a rule, re-equipment on modern lines must be preceded by financial consolidation, and if the industry in question is very diversified, the problem often seems to be insoluble. There are so many rivalries, so many soft jobs, and so many vested interests, all thriving on the common ruin. The axe must be applied by outside influence. As we have seen, when the heavy industries came even partially under the control of the banks, they were no longer able to resist the consolidation dictated by high finance.

As a result of the advances which they are unable to repay, possibly half the cotton industry, a quarter of the woollen industry, and a third of iron, steel, and coal, are now almost reduced to a state of servitude. By threatening them with bankruptcy, their creditors can force on them any form of reorganization they wish, so that the cure is found in the very excess of their ills. During the past few years important industrial reorganizations have been carried out under the aegis of the banks. The banks are thus assuming an initiative which they have not sought, and which certainly did not belong to them in the past.

This vast reform is falling more and more under the financial direction of the Bank of England, for having been won over to the American doctrine of managed currency, she is bravely struggling to maintain part of the manufacturing industry from collapse, just as in the monetary upheaval she is struggling to withstand the excessive gold exports. The establishment by the Bank of the Securities Management Trust in 1930, under the guidance of leading economic experts, is in line with this policy, and is destined to make the Bank the inspiration, the intermediary, and finally the arbitrator of industrial consolidations. That a considerable proportion of British industry is falling under the control of the Bank of England, and therefore of the City, is a grave sign of the times that is inclined to worry the extreme element. Some fear that it may lead to the development of a vast financial community, which, by undertaking industrial reorganization, will obtain control of production and set up an irresistible dictatorship.

In this aspect of the crisis and its solution, we touch upon one of the fundamental divisions of political and economic thought. No matter what the attitude may be, every one can be labelled either as *laissez-faire* or intervention, the two diametrically opposed schools of thought. The non-interventionists, who still cling to the methods of classical Liberalism, do not ask for any exceptional measures for the public good. They are still optimistic enough to hope that the tide will turn and refloat the stranded ship. Meanwhile, even when the waters are at their lowest ebb, they put their complete trust in private enterprise. In spite of the surgical nature of her activities, the Bank definitely belongs to this school, for she hopes to save industry by reorganization, not by legislation.

The theories of the interventionists are the exact opposite. They are steeped, often unwillingly, in commercial and socialistic ideas, which are fundamentally pessimistic and lazy. They look to the State for the necessary effort, for they believe that no satisfactory solution can be found without exceptional measures on the part of the Government. Hence the many suggested panaceas, which keep reappearing with increasing emphasis as the period of difficulty is prolonged: the vast loans destined to stimulate production; "safeguarding," *i.e.* a tariff to protect the home market; Imperial Preference, or even Empire Free Trade; and finally, inflation, the morphine which it is proposed to inject into the worn-out economic tissues. The champions of these various remedies can be distinguished from the partisans of economic Liberalism, for in the field of political intervention they are all eager to "get something done." What invalid can resist a doctor, or even a charlatan, who assures him that he can be cured by some new and infallible remedy?

A man's attitude on this subject depends on his temperament, on something deep down in his innermost being. Any chart of public opinion becomes complicated as each political party includes under a

common heading individuals with opposite tempera-
ments. Among the Conservatives, Lord Beaverbrook
is an interventionist, but Mr. Baldwin, though also
an interventionist, is fundamentally an unwilling
one; in the Labour Party, Sir Oswald Mosley is
an interventionist, while Ramsay MacDonald, and
above all Snowden, are not; finally, in the Liberal
Party, Lloyd George is ready to recommend government expedients of any sort, whereas Sir Herbert
Samuel and Lord Grey at the bottom of their hearts
object to any departure from the true faith.

In so far as she preserves her economic sanity,
England still remains attached by nature as well as
by tradition to the theory of individual initiative and
liberty, which is deep-rooted in her character. This
is being modified, however, by the present tragic
depression, coming as it does after a period of forty
years, during which the ardour of economic conquest has been surreptitiously replaced by the spirit
of defence. The number of the interventionists is
growing daily, with a rapidity which no one could
have foreseen even at the time of the Armistice.

2. INFLATION

There is one way of reducing real wages without touching nominal wages, and that is by raising the general level of prices. World inflation would produce such a result, and England would like to see certain foreign banks of issue collaborating with her to this end. This amounts to a managed currency, international in scope, and capable of serving British interests. If the owners of the gold do not agree to this policy, as is quite probable, England could achieve the same result, by simply inflating her own currency, at any rate in so far as her own economy is concerned. This would counteract, at least partially, the effect of the increase in the value of the pound sterling. In periods of falling prices, wages remain fixed at higher levels and weigh heavily on industry. In rising periods, on the contrary, the same sluggishness retards the increase in wages, and so aids production. Everything is then plain sailing for the employer. He manufactures at low cost, especially if his costs are expressed in gold, for his real wages have been insidiously reduced, while he sells with ease to a public whose purchasing power has been artificially inflated. He exports whatever he likes, for no foreigner can steal unawares into his home market. Unfortunately, such conditions do not last, but in the meantime the manufacturer reaps easy profits. Almost every Continental country had this experience since the War.

British manufacturers are now bewailing the present deplorable situation, but how is it that they have not yet been tempted to imitate the "depreciated currency" policy of so many of their Continental competitors? They are apt to overlook the misery that this policy entails, and sees only the attractions of a monetary drug which gives such elasticity to the business world, wipes out debt, and automatically reduces real wages at the very moment that the workman, not without satisfaction, believes that his wage is being increased. The policy of bringing the pound back to par produced exactly the opposite effect.

An avowed inflationist is hardly to be found in any country. The nearest approach is the man who declares that one must be prudent, very prudent in this matter of deflation. In England this attitude is still the rule, for apart from a few inventors of panaceas, no one openly advocates the systematic depreciation of the pound sterling, although in certain industrial circles one meets an unorganized, almost an unformulated desire for what is virtually the equivalent. They sigh for kindlier treatment, as the monetary policy up to date has been merciless. The following document is significant: "The present depression is largely due to the persistent fall in prices, which the monetary policy has entirely failed to correct. The gold standard has not operated internationally in a healthy way. The bringing of the pound sterling to its pre-War level of gold value, created numerous difficulties of the gravest character for British industries. It automatically increased the real cost of wages and fixed charges. His Majesty's Government is urged to take action on the monetary question without delay, and with the guiding principle that the well-being of British industry is of more vital importance to the people of the country than any financial consideration." [1]

What is the meaning of this, and above all, from the Manchester Chamber of Commerce! Since 1923 doubts have been voiced by certain other industrial circles, and especially by the Federation of British Industries, concerning the wisdom of the prevailing

---

[1] Memorandum of the Manchester Chamber of Commerce to the Prime Minister on the Monetary Policy, 16th September 1930.

monetary policy. Under existing circumstances, one sees more clearly every day that the policy of maintaining the pound sterling at par is crushing the manufacturer.

What exactly do these desires imply? If the pound had been stabilized at a lower level, the nation's burden no doubt would have been lighter, but how is one to seize the exact moment for such stabilization? Who today would undertake to depreciate the pound deliberately, and then stop it at the right point in its decline? Such an attempt might well spell disaster, and would certainly mean the ruin of London as the financial centre of the world. Would any one ever again be willing to hold pounds sterling, or even to make an international contract in pounds? Such counsels of despair are not openly advocated, although there are many who wish to obtain, without actual depreciation, all the advantages that depreciation entails. The idea is thus finally expressed in a roundabout form.

The proposal for an enormous State loan, destined to stimulate both production and consumption, keeps reappearing with growing insistence. It has been championed by both Mr. Lloyd George and Sir Oswald Mosley, neither of whom has won over his political party to the idea. Others, especially where the banking world is allied to industry, prefer a policy of easy money, although a high bank rate is occasionally required to defend the pound sterling. The idea of a sensational loan has not succeeded up to the present, but the policy of borrowing, though only in latent form, has tended to slip unobtrusively into the financial structure of the country. According to the methods of financing unemployment insurance, the fund is able to meet its obligations only while the number of unemployed remains at about 1¼ millions, and above this figure payments are met by Treasury advances. The money so distributed is obtained neither by contributions from the insured, nor by special taxation. Therefore it has somewhat the same effect on consumption and production as the Mosley-Lloyd George policy of government loans.

These obscure desires and vague regrets are no more than the instinctive longings of an invalid seeking relief from pain. Yet the pressure is there, and must be reckoned with. Certain politicians, usually only on the outskirts of their party, do not hesitate to advocate these policies, but a sure instinct restrains the more responsible elements. It would un-

doubtedly lead to the disintegration of the country
if she consented to let the international character
of her money be questioned, or if she renounced
those ideas of credit that have been the backbone
of her system.

3. PROTECTION

Another method of reducing real wages is by a
tariff. It would raise prices, at any rate in the home
market, and a larger share of the proceeds would go
to profits in comparison with wages. For this argument to be acceptable, wages should not be increased,
or at any rate not in the same proportion as prices.
Such is certainly the underlying motive, even though
the system may be presented to the working class as
being the best guarantee of their standard of living.
It is in this sense that doctrinaire free traders like
Mr. Snowden argue that protection is merely a
hypocritical attack on wages.

England exports 25 per cent. to 30 per cent. of
her production; three or four of her principal industries sell abroad anywhere from 40 per cent. to
80 per cent. of their output. At first sight the protectionist solution seems unworkable, since the problem is to preserve or recapture the international

markets. It would seem that this can be done only by lowering the cost of production, after which foreign competition in the home market ceases to be dangerous. At the same time one must point out that raising the level of internal prices, which is the object of protection, places a fresh burden on the export trades. To sacrifice international markets in order to save the home market is an admission of defeat, and a confession that the country has passed from the offensive to the defensive.

The public is well aware of these arguments, and so are the protectionists, but one gathers that the latter are simply concentrating on immediate needs. "It is all very well to talk of exports," they reply, "while the home market is being invaded." There is nothing new in invasion, however, for it dates back to the last ten years of the nineteenth century, when German competition first began to make itself felt. It is since then, and especially since the War, that pressure from without has increased so ominously. In certain lines England has come to rely more and more on imported manufactures, which is contrary to her structure and to her tradition. In 1899, for example, the import of iron and steel amounted to only 645,000 tons against an export of 3,368,000

tons. By 1929 these imports had increased to
2,817,000 tons against a corresponding export of
4,379,000 tons; the proportion of imports to exports
has thus risen from 19 per cent. to 64 per cent.

The same occurs in several other industries,
where the capacity of resistance seems to have weakened. Between 1924 and 1929 the imports of cotton
goods (after deducting re-exports) was increased
from £6,737,000 to £10,173,000; of electrical equipment from £3,211,000 to £6,281,000, and of paper
and cardboard from £14,170,000 to £17,701,000. If
we transpose the 1929 figures to the basis of the
1924 prices which were much higher, the increase in
imports appears still greater, and brings the purchases of cotton goods up to £13,358,000, of electrical equipment to £7,779,000 and of paper and
cardboard up to £22,046,000. As for iron and steel,
imports were £22,024,000 in 1924 and £24,449,000
in 1929, the latter figure being £30,536,000 if we
alter it to the 1924 level.

In view of these figures, it is easy to understand
the instinctive reaction of people who, without looking ahead, think first of protecting themselves by
closing the door. This is the real basis of the English
protectionist movement. Other arguments come

later, some very pertinent ones being based on most seductive scientific considerations, but they seem to have been dug up as an afterthought, and are not considered particularly convincing by their exponents. For example, they contend that under present conditions of mass production a protected home market for part of the output at least creates a stability which assists technical organization, and ensures lower costs. There is also the belief that exports are tending to become a form of regulator, and that the manufacturer would be prepared to lose money on his exports at times, his steady profits being assured by his national *clientèle*. Protection is thus judged to be more capable of stimulating industrial progress than is any other policy. On the other hand, we must not ignore the fact that by perpetuating outworn equipment which ought to be scrapped, protection can retard the programme of consolidation and rationalization. This has all been said by the free traders, but it has fallen on deaf ears, for the public is bored with free trade when the rest of the world, without exception, is indulging in the most shameless orgy of protection and dumping.

Protection has filtered through the entire British structure. In 1914 free trade was still intact, for though its merits had been questioned, in the pre-War customs tariff there was not the slightest departure from Gladstonian Liberalism. Fiscal duties did exist, it is true, but they were not contrary to the doctrine, and none were of a protectionist nature. Even in 1915, when the famous MacKenna duties on motor cars, bicycles, musical instruments, watches, cinema films, etc., were voted, this first serious attack was not intended to act as a protection against outside competition. The object was simply to reduce the import of luxuries in order to assist the overburdened merchant marine, and also to defend the pound sterling against an exceptionally unfavourable trade balance.

Nevertheless these duties did serve as a tariff, and although originally intended only as War measures, they were kept on. The 1921 protection against dumping and against the competition of countries with depreciated exchanges was not maintained, but this was chiefly due to the technical difficulty in its application. The protection of the key industries was introduced in the same year, also as part of the War policy, and since then it has become one of the main features of the English tariff system. In 1921 the Dyestuffs Act was voted for a period of ten years, and was renewed for one year in 1931 only after considerable argument. The dye industry has already benefited greatly from this total prohibition. The 1925 tariff on raw silk gave real protection to artificial silk, and similarly the tariff on hydrocarbon oil resulted in protection for the synthetic benzol produced in England.

Over and above such special measures applying only to these particular articles, the general practice of safeguarding has grown up. This law was instituted in 1921, suspended in 1924, and renewed in 1925. It allowed protection to be granted, after an enquiry had been made by the Board of Trade, to any industry that made application. The main principles of this Act have inspired the tariff policy of the country, in so far as industrial products are concerned. A temporary but renewable tariff of 33⅓ per cent. was granted to a number of industries—lace, wrapping paper, translucent pottery, buttons, enamelled household goods, etc.—but the list is subject to change. The protection granted to gas mantles, cutlery, and fabric gloves, came to an end in 1930, as it was not renewed by the Labour Government then in power. In spite of the precautions taken, such as the fact that there was no general tariff, and that the duties were temporary and strictly limited to individual cases, safeguarding undoubtedly is a form of protection. It frankly sets out to protect national industries against the unfair competition of those who, thanks to lower wages, produce at much lower prices.

The development of English protection, however, does not stop here, for in other less noticeable forms its spirit has penetrated a host of official practices. Many restrictions have been made on imports by order either of the police or the Department of Health, and the Office of Works gives preference to contractors using British materials. According to the Merchandise Marks Act passed in 1926, certain articles coming from abroad must be labelled with their country of origin, either when they are brought into Great Britain or when they are put on sale by the retailer. Under the same heading comes the campaign to "Buy British Goods," which urges the consumer to buy British products simply because they are British. All these are forms of protection in disguise. Though the country has remained faithful in principle to its Liberal traditions, the atmosphere has changed. In the old days imports were hailed by the orthodox school as a sign of wealth, but now to

a host of people, they are an insult not to be tolerated.

Many of these measures, fiscal and otherwise, are
the work of men who do not consider themselves
protectionists, but declare that they still adhere in
principle to free trade. The hypercritical term of
"safeguarding" does not deceive any one; it is
merely the homage rendered by "vicious" protection
to "virtuous" Liberalism. It was long before protection dared show its face openly. At first only secondary trades of little importance solicited the benefit
of safeguarding, but little by little as the depression
grew worse, certain fundamental exporting industries grew accustomed to the idea of taking shelter
behind a tariff. If the Baldwin Cabinet had not been
overthrown in 1929, wool and steel would have
asked for, and no doubt would have obtained, a
tariff. The cotton industry, that last stronghold
of free trade, finally yielded in its turn in 1930. In
other words, protectionist ideas have penetrated
to the very heart of England. It may be only a
fit of temporary discouragement owing to the
unprecedented depression, but the change is incontestable.

England, indeed, has altered out of all recognition. Any one who knew the country in the nineteenth century or even at the beginning of the twentieth, remembers how free trade was then upheld as an unquestioned dogma. It had passed from the domain of business where it belonged, into that of sentiment. It was a religion, and even to analyze it was sacrilege. In 1903, when Joseph Chamberlain first dared to break away from this unanimous reverence, he was greeted with a positive outcry, in which even moral condemnation was included. It has taken over twenty years as well as a formidable War, and a no-less tragic trade depression, to induce the British public to look upon the tariff problem as a practical discussion of self-interest—which is really all it amounts to!

When the younger generation is not actually protectionist, it is still interventionist in mentality, which indicates a significant change in the spirit of the country. The people have lost their old orthodox ideas. They do not seem hostile to free trade, yet one can hardly call them convinced, active Liberals. The evolution dates back to the early years of the century, and applies to most men under forty years of age. The political atmosphere is completely transformed, for it is now difficult to arouse the enthu-

siasm of a British audience by taking free trade, as
it is no longer a question of faith.

This is particularly so amongst the workmen,
especially members of the trade unions. Their attitude is not surprising, as it merely brings to light
a very old tendency. Since the unions were first
formed, the basis of their programme has been the
protection of the nation's labour. Tariff protection
is only another aspect of the same political conception, which both admits and requests the intervention of the State. Though English labour leaders
have been subjected to Gladstonian influences for
several generations, today they are becoming the
defenceless prey of protectionist propaganda, and
their flocks are even more susceptible. In every industry the workmen discuss the eventuality of a
tariff in a matter-of-fact way. All they ask is that
industrial activity should be maintained, and the
risk of unemployment reduced. In the enquiries
made by the Board of Trade following requests for
safeguarding, it was found that the workmen nearly
always favoured a tariff. It is curious to note that
their protectionism is so instinctive and unconscious,
that among them one often meets men who declare
they are free traders, and yet naïvely advocate an

import quota or even total prohibition, without for a moment suspecting that they are being inconsistent!

This does not mean that the masses are no longer influenced by certain powerful Liberal arguments. When the country comes face to face with an increase in the cost of living, which is an inevitable consequence of protection, it is bound to take fright, especially in the North. It was in this practical, hard-headed mood that the protectionist suggestions of the first Baldwin Cabinet were turned down in the 1923 election. Not that it was anything like the protest of the electors in 1906, when Chamberlain and his proposed wheat tax were swept out in a veritable landslide. At that time, quite apart from the fear of dear bread, there was an irresistible wave of Cobdenite sentiment. Today, the epithet "Cobden-ite" is frequently applied in derision to a man who is not progressive, who is not abreast of the times. The real insular nature of the British is just as apparent in their present objection to foreign goods, as in the days of international expansion in the last generation. Anything foreign is still instinctively considered *bizarre* and even suspect.

These reasons are sufficient explanation of the undoubted progress made by protection in both

Labour and capitalist circles. At its meeting on 26th June 1930, the Council of Trades Union Congress openly advocated an Imperial policy which meant the abandonment of free trade. For some time the Federation of British Industries has also been travelling along the same road, as was clearly shown by a referendum amongst its members in October 1930. Only 3.9 per cent. of the replies were in favour of retaining the present tariff policy, 96.1 per cent. demanded a change, *i.e.* some form of a tariff, and not a single industrial group gave a majority in favour of continuing free trade. The Manchester Chamber of Commerce itself registered the same tendency in its referendum taken in July 1930: 1736 votes were for protection, against 607 for free trade, and also, as might be expected in Manchester, there were 1600 abstentions. Lancashire, the adopted motherland of Cobden, is evidently tainted. In our efforts to gauge the direction in which British industry is moving, we now know the verdict.

Even the City, the last fortress of *laissez-faire,* has let its free trade faith be tampered with. Although it made a reservation adhering to the principle of free trade, the Banker's Manifesto of 4th July 1930 admitted that England should hold herself ready to place a tariff on all foreign goods, exceptions, naturally, being made in favour of Imperial trade. I could hardly believe my eyes when I read this declaration over the signatures of the great financiers and merchants of the City. Evidently, they also are weary of waiting for the international economic disarmament which never comes. Perhaps also their attitude can be explained by the fact that the City has surreptitiously changed in character. Previously, the Cunliffe Committee, which was exclusively recruited from finance, imposed a monetary policy of its own choice on an industry with which it was not closely allied. Today these same industries are in debt to the banks, who are directing their reorganization. The banks have, therefore, become partially industrialized, and accordingly they adopt a train of thought which applies more to production than to trade. Several of these neo-protectionists, who were enumerated and qualified in *The Times* of 10th July, at the time of the manifesto, are really more industrialists than bankers.

This preoccupation with immediate domestic interests instead of international affairs, is already felt in political circles. "Scratch a Conservative," Lord Salisbury loved to say, "and you will find a

protectionist." This latent tendency, which the old
statesman of the nineteenth century already suspected, is plainly visible today. With varying shades
of opinion, the Conservative forces have now rallied
to a policy of safeguarding and tariffs. The party
will hesitate, no doubt, before imposing a tax on
food, for memories are bitter on this point, but the
advocates of industrial protection pure and simple
can entirely rely upon its support. The Conservative
leader has several times clearly stated this programme: Protection of national industry against
foreign competition—a thorough-going policy of
safeguarding; the introduction of special taxes
against dumping; the employment of reprisals as a
weapon in negotiations ("I want to retaliate on
people who hit us. . . ."); the development of a
British preference in the Empire markets.

In 1900 the Conservative Party, as I knew it, was
almost unanimously free trade, but today the last
supporters have been won over. In 1923 Lord Derby,
a Lancashire man, was torn between his faith in
economic freedom and his loyalty to the Conservative Party. His struggle with his conscience was
quite impressive. "I am a free trader," he said, "and
always have been, but . . ." In other words, even

against his convictions, he agreed that certain concessions were necessary. Today, this truly representative man, who stands for the most solid and serious elements in Old England, declared in 1930, quite simply, in a speech at Liverpool: "I was raised in the free trade faith. I have been a free trader all my life. I am one no longer. I think that, up to a certain point, foreign markets are lost for us, and some of them we will never regain. We therefore must do all in our power to protect our own home market. I am a fervent partisan of a policy of legitimate safeguarding carefully worked out. . . ."

It is interesting to study the psychology of the Labour Party, whose chiefs were brought up as free traders in the Liberal school. In several cases their faith is vacillating, for the temptations of protection are being insinuated through the trade unions as well as through other channels. It would be difficult for the Conservative Party alone to introduce a tariff, but with the help, or at any rate the tacit consent of Labour, the position is modified, and without doubt it will be only in this way that the national attitude can be altered after a century of the opposite policy. Moreover, we need only go back to their distant origins to realize that neither the descendants

of the Tories nor the first trade unionists owed any
fidelity to Cobden's dogma.

This is not true of the Liberal Party, however,
but even here the poison has penetrated to the very
heart. How has this pure gold been transmuted into
base metal? Today we find two essential underlying
forces in Liberalism: Nonconformist sentiment, and
orthodox economist philosophy. The majority of
the Nonconformist flock is now passing over to
Labour, and as for the economists of the Liberal
Party, are they still genuine believers in *laissez-
faire?* After all, one can hardly expect a leader like
Mr. Lloyd George to be orthodox. In 1930 certain
noted Liberals even suggested the establishment of
a uniform tariff of 10 per cent. on all imports.

4. CONCLUSION

The time is now ripe for an experiment with a
policy renouncing traditional free trade, though perhaps I would not be justified in saying more. The old
resistance to protection that won the day ever since
the first attacks made by Joseph Chamberlain in
1903 is now over. The tax on raw materials and
foodstuffs remains in abeyance, in view of the Empire Free Trade movement, and possibly it will never

be achieved. But safeguarding, *i.e.* the protection of industrial goods in the home market, is virtually accomplished. The danger of this attitude is that once again it draws attention away from the real fundamental cause of the present depression. It overlooks the flaws in the international economic equilibrium, which a self-contained unit like the United States, or even a partially self-supporting country like France, may possibly ignore, but which England, dependent on foreign trade, cannot neglect for long without mortal danger to her very existence.

The bold solution would have been to reduce prices at all costs, but perhaps this would have been impossible with a policy of appreciated money. It is rather feeble, though, to try to consolidate wages behind a tariff barrier and at the same time to raise the level of domestic prices if possible. Viewed in this light, British protection exceeds the framework of any one class or any one group of interests. Basically, it protects one system of prices against other systems of prices, each arising out of different monetary policies, and different conceptions of material comfort. By thus clutching at a standard of living that is much higher than that of the rest of Europe, England may make it still more difficult to export to these countries, and it may mean the abandonment, at least partially, of her policy of un- restricted international relations. One wonders anx- iously whether the destiny of Great Britain lies in that direction.

This renunciation, for such it is, is only the ac- ceptance of a new British status. Formerly, the policy of exporting capital as well as goods was of first importance, for the expatriated capital acted the part of a pioneer, but latterly the income from for- eign investments seems to have been used to pay for the excess of imports, in other words, part of the people's food. The prominence of exports in the system has thus declined, and from the industrial point of view the home market has become more de- sirable. If this is the case, protection, which was anathema to the last generation, can now be justified by serious arguments, the best being that it should be given a fair trial.

CHAPTER VIII

IMPERIAL PREFERENCE

I. BRITISH VS. IMPERIAL TRADE

THE British export trade may have diminished in relative importance in the national balance sheet, but it is still by far the most influential factor. It is impossible to conceive of England without her exports. What is even more significant, however, is that she is depending to an increasing extent on the outside world, for only 56.7 per cent. of her food was produced at home in the period of 1923-28 as compared with 59.5 per cent. in 1909-13. In the case of wheat the figure today is only 21 per cent. In the last analysis the great volume of imports can be paid for only by exports, and any expedient which does not take this into account is bound to be still-born.

How far can England rely upon the Empire, either as a purveyor or as a market? The food supply seemed to be the outstanding necessity at the time of the War and up to 1920, but during the present period of over-production, attention is being concentrated on the export markets, as their loss is the chief cause of the depression in England. Under the circumstances can the Empire possibly come to the rescue of the Mother Country?

We must distinguish between Imperial Trade and British trade, for their destinies are by no means the same.[1] Between 1913 and 1927 Imperial trade, including transactions between various parts of the Empire, increased by 27 per cent., although world trade increased by only 20 per cent. The Empire's share in the world's total, increased from 27.75 per cent. to 29.48 per cent. In the total volume of Imperial trade, however, the transactions with the rest of the world are more important than those within the Empire itself, the proportion being 61 per cent. and 39 per cent. respectively. These proportions have scarcely changed since the War. Obviously, this complex commonwealth cannot lightly set about constituting itself a closed economic group.

If, for the sake of argument, we consider the Empire as a single unit, we find that its foreign trade contrasts as follows with the rest of the world:

[1] Report of Imperial Economic Committee, 13th Report, commonly called Sir David Chadwick's Report, 1930: A memorandum on the trade of the British Empire, 1913, 1925, 1928.

PROPORTION OF EMPIRE TRADE IN TOTAL
WORLD TRADE

	1913	1927
British Empire	18.86%	20.28%
Northern and Western Europe	38.40	31.07
United States	12.54	16.06
Rest of the World	30.20	32.59

The Empire's share has thus increased slightly, the United States considerably, but Europe has declined. In so far as the Empire itself is concerned, however, inter-Empire trade has diminished relatively, and extra-Empire trade has increased. This is partly accounted for by the fact that many products that were previously shipped to England for re-export, are now routed direct. Thus the entrepôt aspect is becoming less important than the shipment of goods for immediate consumption—in other words, a centrifugal force is at work.

If we now consider the relative progress of the various parts of the Empire, we find the rates of evolution differ greatly:

INCREASE IN IMPORTS

	1913	1927
Great Britain and Northern Ireland	100%	114%
Canada, India, South Africa, New Zealand	100	126
United States	100	180
The World as a Whole	100	122

INCREASE IN EXPORTS

	1913	1927
Great Britain and Northern Ireland	100%	79%
Canada, India, South Africa, New Zealand	100	131
United States	100	157
The World as a Whole	100	118

This is the very heart of the problem. England is not behindhand in the matter of absorbing imports, as we have already seen, but in exports she has definitely declined, although her Dominions as a group have progressed more quickly than the world as a whole. This emphasizes the diverging destinies of a prosperous Empire, and a mother country no longer prosperous like her European neighbours. Britain is suffering from old age, whereas her Empire shares in the youth of the New World. It may, indeed, be useless for the England of today to try to cut herself adrift from the rest of Europe.

Let us carry the analysis further and examine the origin of the imports of the overseas Empire and the destination of its exports, as this discloses the real place that England occupies in the commercial activity of her Empire.

ORIGIN OF IMPORTS INTO THE OVERSEAS EMPIRE

Coming from	1913	1927
Great Britain and Northern Ireland	44.2%	36.1%
Other parts of the Empire	11.5	13.1
Foreign Countries	44.3	50.8

DESTINATION OF EXPORTS FROM THE OVERSEAS EMPIRE

Going to	1913	1927
Great Britain and Northern Ireland	41.2%	36.8%
Other parts of the Empire	10.6	10.7
Foreign Countries	48.2	52.5

The Mother Country undoubtedly remains the economic centre, although the tendency of the Overseas Empire is to deal less with her and more with foreign countries in imports as well as exports. Here again a centrifugal force is at work.

Once more the divergence of destiny is apparent, for the foreign commerce of Great Britain shows exactly the opposite trend.

ORIGIN OF BRITISH IMPORTS [1]

	1913	1927
Coming from the Empire	20.5%	27.0%
Coming from Foreign Countries	79.5	73.0

DESTINATION OF BRITISH EXPORTS

	1913	1927
Going to the Empire	37.2%	43.2%
Going to Foreign Countries	62.8	56.8

These figures disclose a startling situation. While England's share in Imperial trade is diminishing,

[1] The 1913 figures are for the United Kingdom, and those for 1927 for Great Britain and Northern Ireland.

the share of the Empire in England's trade is on the increase. This means that the Mother Country's dealings are less widely distributed geographically, whereas the trade of the Overseas Empire is more so. Colonial trade has expanded while that of the Mother Country has contracted. The Empire looks less towards England, but England looks more towards the Empire; the Old Country seems to be taking refuge behind her young offspring. Between 1913 and 1927, imports coming into Great Britain from the Empire increased by 41 per cent., but those from foreign countries by only 15 per cent.; during the same period her exports to foreign countries were reduced by 29 per cent., but those to the Empire by only 9 per cent.

In view of the relative fidelity of the Imperial customer—a phenomenon which was also observed during the depression at the close of the nineteenth century—we can understand that the English are apt to forget that nearly three-fifths of their exports are still directed towards international markets. Naturally, the Empire is a powerful attraction.

"The foreigner is abandoning us," they think. "Very well. Let us turn towards our kinsmen, who live and think as we do, and among whom we will find not only goodwill but preferential tariff treatment. We have been faithful too long to the old orthodox formulae, according to which one must buy in the cheapest market and sell in the dearest. In a world that is closing itself against us, is it not better to look for the most dependable source of supply, and the most faithful customer?"

Following the line of least resistance, England is now turning wearily to the colonies which she created in the hey-day of her youth. As old age approaches, she is tempted to rely upon them as a father will rely upon his vigorous sons. One can quote endless statistics in proof of this attitude. In 1929 the United States, Britain's most important foreign customer, took 6.57 per cent. of her exports, whereas India took 11.28 per cent. and Australia 7.82 per cent. It is true that 52 per cent. of her exports of manufactured goods are sold to foreign countries, but some of her most important industries do the majority of their trade within the Empire: paper, 74 per cent.; knit goods, 72 per cent.; electrical equipment, 61 per cent.; motor cars and carriages, 59 per cent.; pottery, 58 per cent.; woodwork, 55 per cent.; hardware, 55 per cent. Other industries, no less important, depend on the Imperial

market, if not for the majority of their exports, at
any rate for a large proportion which could not be
replaced, such as silk, for example, with 49 per cent.,
engineering with 47 per cent., cotton goods with 44
per cent., woollens with 32 per cent. Finally, although the population of the Dominions is relatively
small, the purchasing power *per capita* is considerable, especially where British products are concerned. In 1929 every New Zealander bought £14,
11s. 1d. worth from England, every Australian £8,
10s. 2d., and every South African £4, 3s. 8d. The
corresponding figures for foreign countries are:
Norway, £3, 10s. 7d.; Argentina, £2, 12s. 10d.;
France, 15s. 5d.; and America, 7s. 6d.

That the Empire's share in the total British exports is undeniably greater today than it was before
the War, is proved by the following table:

DESTINATION OF BRITISH EXPORTS

	1913	1927	1928	1929
To Foreign Countries ...	62.8%	57.4%	58.0%	59.0%
To the Empire	37.2	42.6	42.0	41.0

As these figures show, the Empire has been taking
about two-fifths of Britain's exports since the War,
instead of about one-third as in 1913. This fact has

been so impressed on the public by a campaign of propaganda, that people seem to forget that these proportions may possibly arise from exceptional circumstances. Actually, the Empire's share in British exports has decreased slightly since 1927. Europe, meanwhile, is rapidly regaining her former place among British customers, thanks to the restoration of her purchasing power to the 1913 level. Referring to the recent changes in British trade, a well-known economist writes as follows: "We have held our position better in Europe than elsewhere, and better in the British Empire than in other parts of the trans-oceanic continents." [1] He gives the Empire only second place, and this is a significant fact which is still too new to have had any influence as yet on political or even on economic thought, especially as during the last few years attention has been entirely concentrated on the Imperial point of view.

In a crisis all thoughts naturally turn towards the Empire. If England is to get sympathy, help, and privileged treatment from her Empire, therein may lie the germ of a possible solution which we cannot

[1] A. Loveday, "Britain and World Trade," *The Economist,* Monthly Supplement, 25th October 1930.

afford to neglect. There is nothing new in this, for as far back as the depression of 1880 we find the same idea, and since then it has been brought up at regular intervals by such men as Farrer Ecroyd, Lord Randolph Churchill, and Joseph Chamberlain.

Since the War there has been a steady growth of interest in the conception of a British Empire, more or less closed to the rest of the world and capable of rescuing the Old Country from her depression. Now is the time to show oneself a realist. What exactly can be expected from the Empire? Is the Empire willing to entertain such a programme? Out of the 41 per cent. of the British exports that went to the Empire, the Dominions in 1929 took 20.8 per cent., India 11.3 per cent., and the Crown colonies 8.9 per cent. How much goodwill can England count upon from them, especially from those which have developed beyond her control? How far can she rely upon their help? The Empire is no longer modelled upon the Colonial Pact, in which the Mother Country dominated, nor yet on the nineteenth-century plan, in which she still directed. It is now regarded as a group of "autonomous communities within the British Empire, equal in status, in no way subordinate one to another in any aspect of their domestic or external affairs."[1] Under the present conditions of the Empire, these questions are of primary importance.

2. WHAT BRITAIN CAN EXPECT FROM THE DOMINIONS

The Dominions all acknowledge the British tie and allegiance to the Crown, but with varying degrees of enthusiasm. Australia and New Zealand are faithful by sentiment, but also by self-interest; Canada is loyal at heart, but independent in attitude and geographically American; South Africa is divided and doubtful in its attachment; India, which we shall classify in this group for convenience, is hostile, and to a certain extent so is Ireland, though bound in many respects by economic interest. Whatever these feelings may amount to, the unity of the system is maintained by sentiment, and even more by acquiescence in the fact that they are all part of the same Empire—this last is a force which foreigners are apt to neglect or underestimate.

Coinciding with this acquiescence is an intransi-

[1] These are the terms used in the Report of the Imperial Conference, 1926.

gent desire for independence in each of the Dominions, though its expression and tone vary considerably. In this, Ireland is to a certain extent the
ringleader, making the most of every circumstance
with a lack of restraint which at times amounts to
sabotage. In spite of minorities who are passionately
British and deplore these tendencies, Canada and
South Africa never miss an opportunity of proclaim-
ing their independence, having it publicly stated,
acknowledged, and increased. Australia, too, likes
to have her independence acknowledged, but she
willingly accommodates herself to the existing state
of affairs. Only New Zealand is completely satisfied.
This brief review indicates the geographical distribution of both the Conservative and progressive
schools of thought.

When England is confronted with her youthful
partners, who have now come of age and have lost
even their feelings of deference towards her, she
finds herself appealing to a most incongruous set
of loyalties. Economic interest, however, is always
there and where the Dominions rely almost entirely
on England as a market for their export trade, they
are bound to her by an exceedingly solid tie. It is in
England that New Zealand finds 78.9 per cent. of her

overseas customers; South Africa 54.4 per cent.; and Ireland 96.8 per cent. Australia, on the other hand, with 40.7 per cent., Canada with 35.4 per cent., and India with 22.5 per cent., are less exclusively tied down, although even these proportions are heavy. The British market gives them all an ideal outlet for their raw materials. Canada and Australia export their wheat; Australia and New Zealand their meat; Australia, New Zealand, and South Africa, their wool; India its wheat, rice, and cotton. Except for Canada, which is steadily exporting more manufactured goods, the Dominions are all complementary to an industrialized Great Britain, and this even applies to Canada, in so far as she, too, sells raw materials.

Another factor of economic dependence, no less important, is that the Empire finds in the Mother Country its main source of capital, for when the Dominion Governments wish to borrow they naturally turn to London. Canada has been completely absorbed in the American orbit, having now only 11 per cent. of her public debt placed in England, but the proportion for Australia, on the other hand, is 48 per cent., for New Zealand 56 per cent., and for South Africa 61 per cent. Australia, though practically in default in 1930, was still able to carry on financially through the help of the City.

Let us not be misled by the solicitous attitude that England often adopts in Imperial discussions. By habit now deeply ingrained, she invariably gives way to her partners' demands without seriously attempting to teach them the reality and the extent of their responsibilities, although they badly need the lesson. The result is that the Mother Country—if such we may still call her—is apt to play the rôle of a reticent old partner who is on the defensive, while the Dominions talk big, insinuate, and dogmatize, in a fashion that they themselves would never tolerate for a moment.

Bearing these things in mind, let us estimate the aid that England, today and in the future, can reasonably expect from the Dominions.

In the first place, she can rely on them for a certain amount of political co-operation, but with many reservations if only English interests, in the narrow sense of the word, are at stake. The aid will be seriously and generously accorded if the whole Empire is affected, or what comes to the same thing, if the Mother Country is in grave danger. Also, she will find unexpected devotion if it comes to a question of defending British civilization from destruction, and even if we suggest that the United States will probably also lend assistance, the value of Dominion aid is in no way diminished.

England can count also on a general economic cooperation, vague, but precious nevertheless, for many activities can be usefully organized on Imperial lines. This is already taking place in the development of communication by wireless, cable, and aviation, in the creation of a unified system of trade marks, and in commercial publicity. Other instances of this are the standardization of certain manufactured articles, and the use of propaganda for stirring up patriotism to buy British products—the Empire Marketing Board urges the English to favour Empire goods, and reciprocal action throughout the Empire would be useful and welcome. Without a doubt the English-speaking peoples of the world have every reason to collaborate. Many Englishmen consider that in this the Americans should be included. At all events, the various parts of the Empire are all members of the same family, and therefore their union means much more than a mere combination of political forces.

Finally, the Mother Country can rely on a certain

amount of customs preference. Canada in 1897 was the first to bestow this privilege on England, and since then her example has been generally followed. The system is carried out by means of a tariff with three levels—an Imperial tariff for England and the rest of the Empire, an intermediary tariff for countries giving reciprocal advantages, and a general tariff for the rest of the world. British products are ordinarily accorded a reduction of about 30 per cent. off the regular tariff; such is the case in Canada and Australia, while New Zealand offers 30 per cent. to 40 per cent. Foreign countries making commercial treaties can obtain about half this preference.

Where the Dominions are less sentimentally inclined, the preference is smaller, and in some cases is singularly precarious. The South African preference amounts to some 25 per cent., but a commercial treaty with Germany—not ratified, it is true—proposed to accord her the full Imperial tariff on certain articles. As a result of an agreement concluded at the Imperial Conference in 1930 this German treaty is not to be ratified, but on the condition, however, that England herself confirms the preferential treatment which the Union of South Africa at present receives from the British tariff.

India, now that she has escaped from British economic influence, grants England only very limited tariff favours. In the past, so long as the Mother Country had absolute control, the Indian tariff was purely fiscal, and an excise duty on cotton taxed the local industry with an amount equivalent to the tax on the imported article from England. Since Indian autonomy has come more or less into existence, England is given a slight advantage over the foreigner, but the Indian manufacturer definitely protects himself against her. On cotton goods, so essential to Manchester, the foreigner pays a 20 per cent. duty, and England only 15 per cent., but the old excise duty of 15 per cent. has been abolished.

The result of these preferential tariffs, all more or less similar, is that the Mother Country enjoys an advantage over the foreigner which is not without value. Nevertheless, all the Dominions have definitely adopted the principle of protecting their own industries, even against British competition, by means of an adequate tariff, and apparently there is a limit below which no amount of co-operation will induce them to go.

3. WHAT BRITAIN CANNOT EXPECT FROM THE DOMINIONS

Every one of the Dominions wishes to give England a preference over the foreigner, but they all consider their own interests first. "Canada first" was adopted as a slogan without embarrassment by the Canadian Government, and although the other Dominions may not express themselves quite so frankly, their outlook is exactly the same. It is generally felt that the local producer, and especially the local manufacturer, should be protected against outside competition; the barrier against the foreigner is often so high as to be almost prohibitive, while against England it is sufficient to give effective protection. No prime minister in any of the Dominions could obtain from parliament or from the electorate a more extensive tariff concession than that.

This form of preference, which is the only one that has been practised, is really of no great importance, for at best it is simply a *régime* of genuine protection. It can, however, be considered a great favour in comparison with the treatment accorded to other countries, against whom the tariff is almost prohibitive. Imperial preference is simply a breach

in the wall, although the wall itself still stands. It is
easy to make eloquent speeches eulogizing mutual
goodwill and the unity of the British Empire. Yet
we must never be so naïve as to forget that the
Dominions must be classed among the most highly
protected countries in the world. At the first sign of
trouble the immediate reaction is to raise the tariff,
and when in their goodwill towards the Mother
Country they wish to maintain the full amount of
her preference, or even augment it, it is always done
by increasing the regular tariff, never by reducing
the Imperial one. This is no real advantage, for,
like the rest of the world, England is suffering from
growing tariff barriers everywhere. In a word, the
colonial manufacturer regards the British manufacturer simply as a competitor, and I know of no subject in which the passage from the enthusiasm of
words to the reality of facts can be so chilly. After
visiting the Empire, one is astonished to find that
a whole section of the English public still considers
Imperial preference as a life-line to which they can
cling.

Periodically the old hope of tariff union crops up
in some Utopian form. Joseph Chamberlain considered it, but he quickly discarded the idea of an

Imperial *zollverein* as being impossible. Nevertheless, from time to time the public keeps harking back to it with a curious persistence. Under the patronage of Lord Beaverbrook, the Empire Free Trade Crusade, which is synonymous with tariff union, aroused the country in 1930. At first sight, no doubt, the idea of surrounding the Empire by a single tariff barrier with complete internal free trade is seductive, but it can be retained only by those who are determined to deceive themselves. It presupposes an economic unity throughout the Empire, which in reality does not exist. To rely on such a programme is merely building castles in the air. It also presupposes that the Dominions will acquiesce, although they have never done so, and have for years formally denied such a possibility. It needed only one sitting of the Imperial Conference in 1930 to prick the bubble so laboriously inflated by the Empire Free Traders. The British public, which has often been blinded by unreasoning optimism, allows itself to be deceived by illusions which, at the approach of reality, are mercilessly dispelled.

We must therefore discard as of no practical value the conception of a complete tariff union, but this does not apply to preference. Out of the discussions of half a century there emerges one incontestable fact, namely, that England can obtain further concessions, but only if she is ready to pay the price. Sentiment, it is true, plays an important part in this persistent desire to co-operate between peoples of the same race and the same language, and it may even be indispensable; but inevitably the time arrives when the discussion centres on self-interest. The Dominions did not demand any counterpart for their first concessions, but, as we have just shown, these turned out to be scarcely concessions at all. When it is a question of anything further, the Dominions demand, either explicitly or otherwise, that England on her side should grant some preference to colonial produce. In the days of Chamberlain the request was merely insinuated and not made directly, but today it is presented with no attempt at concealment.

Now, in order to be worth anything to young countries exporting primary products, a preference in the British market must be on articles of general consumption—on such raw materials and food-stuffs as wool, wheat, and meat. When one gets to grips with the problem, one comes up against this *sine qua non,*—that in order to make this Dominion preference possible, a tariff must first be levied on wheat, meat, and wool coming from abroad. Actually, the discussion is entirely concentrated on wheat.

Since the Imperial Conference of 1887 the problem has literally not gone one step nearer solution, because each negotiator, the Englishman as well as the colonial, wants to get from the other something which will not and cannot be given up. The Mother Country desires colonial markets for her manufactured goods, and therefore she wants a real, not merely a relative, reduction in the tariffs of the Dominions. This, however, is invariably refused. In its turn the Empire wishes to sell food-stuffs and raw materials in the English market, and therefore seeks a tariff preference which free trade England cannot grant without ceasing to be free trade. The British Government, full of goodwill, no doubt does all it can. Since the War, or more exactly, since the 1919 Budget, Dominion preference has been introduced into the tariff on all sorts of secondary articles, such as sugar, wine, dried fruits, etc. But when it comes to wheat, England stops, horrified.

Without a tax on wheat no progress can be made. As far back as 1894, when Lord Jersey represented the British Government at the Colonial Conference in Ottawa, he expressed an attitude to which every responsible leader has since been forced to adhere, unless he is ready to be disowned by the country.[1] "Outside commerce in the United Kingdom," he said, "is made up to three-quarters with foreign countries outside of the Empire. The policy which is proposed to us necessitates a fundamental change in the British policy. As far as the colonies are concerned, it is simply a question of lightly disburdening an existing taxation, but in so far as we are concerned, we should have to create from the start a new tariff." Chamberlain, as Minister for the Colonies, tackled exactly the same problem a few years later. It was at that time, in 1897, that Sir Wilfred Laurier, the initiator of Imperial Preference, made the statement that it would be "necessary for England to advance or Canada would retire." And because he did not wish to run the risk of provoking such a retreat, Chamberlain had the courage in 1903 to propose a tax on wheat and meat, from which colonial imports would be exempt. This created such a sensation that the country's disapproval has never been forgotten, and since then no

[1] Report of Lord Jersey on the Colonial Conference in Ottawa, 21st August 1894.

party leader has dared go before the general electorate with a platform including taxes on the main food products.

This is the present situation. The Imperial Conference of 1930 was hailed by Imperialistic propaganda as the dawn of a new era, and once more the old, old platitudes were unearthed. "The primary concern of Canada today," declared Mr. R. B. Bennett, Prime Minister of that Dominion, in the general discussion on 8th October, "is profitably to sell her wheat. We believe that we shall be reaching towards a solution of that problem if we can establish a better market in Great Britain. This market we want, and for it we are willing to pay by giving in the Canadian market a preference for British goods. . . . First, we must approve or reject the principle. I put the question definitely to you, and definitely it should be answered. There is here no room for compromise and there is no possibility of avoiding the issue. . . . This proposed preference should not be considered as a step towards Empire free trade. In our opinion Empire free trade is neither desirable nor possible."

"I offer to the Mother Country, and to all other parts of the Empire, a preference in the Canadian market in exchange for a like preference in theirs, based upon the addition of a 10 per cent. increase in the prevailing general tariffs or upon tariffs yet to be created." [1]

Once again we have the Dominions rejecting any idea of sacrifice in their minimum tariff, and yet they do not let England forget that nothing can be done in the way of genuine Imperial preference unless she is willing to adopt some general form of protection on her principal food-stuffs. To Mr. Bennett's demand Mr. MacDonald replied in the name of the Labour Government: "Tax wheat: we cannot do it." [2]

It is more than likely that in his position any other prime minister would have said the same thing. All other suggested solutions, however, are simply substitutes. A quota system of imports was proposed, favouring home-grown wheat first, then Imperial, and it looks as if this project will be supported by the Conservatives. It was also proposed that the State should undertake, as it did during the War, the bulk purchase of imports. This would allow a proportion to be reserved for Empire pro-

[1] Speech by R. B. Bennett, 8th October, analytical account in *The Times*, 9th October 1930.
[2] Speech by Ramsay MacDonald in the House of Commons, 28th October 1930.

ducers, and in addition the idea would not frighten the Labour Party. Being unprepared to discuss these eventualities, the conference adjourned without success, in an atmosphere of extreme disappointment—although the result could easily have been foreseen. The British Government did, however, promise to maintain existing preferences for three years, in so far as that can be done constitutionally.

The problem remains unsolved and as thorny as ever. The refusal of the Labour Cabinet does not definitely commit the country, for a matter of such importance cannot be settled without consulting the electorate and giving them an opportunity to say plainly whether they are ready to renounce free trade on wheat in order to strengthen the Imperial tie. This solution appeals to the Conservatives, but they must begin by settling their own attitude. They will have to decide definitely to follow either Mr. Baldwin, who hesitates, or the true protectionists of the Neville Chamberlain type, who do not. This orientation will be decisive. A tax on wheat would mean the reversal of a century-old policy. Also for the first time since the far-off days of the old Colonial Pact, the British horizon would be limited;

England would be imprisoned within a closed system.

4. TO WHAT EXTENT CAN ENGLAND USE THE DOMINIONS?

The Empire markets refuse to allow unconditional entry to the manufactured goods of the Mother Country, and similarly the raw materials from the Dominions cannot be considered as being entirely at the disposal of the British consumer—thus the economic unity of the Empire, though no doubt a latent force, is not an immediate reality. During the War the Dominions willingly allowed wholesale requisitioning of their outputs by England, and in all probability they would do so again, should the Empire collaborate in another English war. In time of peace, however, and even in time of war, as long as no agreement is made, Australian wool is still Australian, and Canadian wheat is still Canadian. Except in the Crown colonies, the raw materials of the Empire are not British in the narrow sense of the term.

Agreement, of course, is always possible between countries speaking the same language, and having the same civilization and the same king, but also

there is nothing to prevent any part of the Empire
from making its own arrangements with foreign
countries. The economic life of Canada, for example,
is full of associations that draw her beyond the
frontier, and carry her towards America without
any possible counteracting influence. To speak Im-
perially of economic unity, therefore, or to add up
the total output of the Empire, as is often done in
order to arrive at a general figure, is very deceptive.
We reasoned in this way during the War, when we
still thought that the resources of the Allies would
indefinitely remain in common.

No doubt a more equitable distribution of the
population could be obtained over all the territory at
the disposal of the Empire, but this territory is no
longer under English control. The Imperialistic
school dwells with irrefutable logic on the present
senseless situation, and points out that the over-
populated Mother Country has nearly four hundred
inhabitants per square mile, whereas Australia has
less than three. They recommend, very properly, a
concerted policy of migration. The Overseas Settlement Committee, established in 1922 by Mr. Amery,
has tried to put this into practice, but the experience
of the last few years proves that in the Empire,

free trade in men is no more successful than free
trade in goods. Australia declares she wants colonists of British origin, but when they are offered,
how mercilessly she sifts this human stream. Canada, although her gates are open wider, shows the
same suspicious attitude. The English emigrant,
humiliated by so many precautions, may well protest with injured pride: "Civis Romanus sum," but
that makes it no easier for him to enter. The Imperial community is often compared with the American community, but this reasoning is false, for
men and products move about within the United
States without restraint or formality.

The same is true even in the case of the English
pro-consuls, of whose services the Dominions no
longer avail themselves. In the nineteenth century
the Mother Country provided magnificent careers
for the energy and talent of her *élite,* by sending
these leaders of men out into the Empire. Today,
however, her *Tu regere imperio populos memento*
applies only to such parts of the Empire as are definitely administrative, though it is true they still
form an immense area. We shall discuss them further in another chapter.

Since the Imperial Conference of 1926, it is no

longer necessary for the governors of the Dominions to be English, and shortly after the 1930 conference, Sir Isaac Isaacs, an Australian, was proposed by the Australian Government as the next Governor-General.

The current has been reversed. It is now the colonies that try to inspire the general policy of the Empire, and even that of England herself. Lord Beaverbrook, for example, is a Canadian, and accordingly he feels and reasons on Imperial matters from the Imperial point of view. Nevertheless, when the Overseas Settlement Committee in London discusses from the English point of view some policy which aims at directing colonists towards Australia, this fact is resented by the Australians as an intrusion into their affairs.

Having thus laid down what the home country can and cannot expect from the Dominions, we should conclude by saying that the latter have almost completely escaped from British control. They adopt towards England the attitude of married sons towards their father. The old man is allowed very little say in the way they run their households. This simile of a family is true to the letter, for we are dealing with the relationship between the parent and the children—the latter are jealous of their majority so recently attained, but the head of the family, pleased with his offspring, says contentedly: "Look what I have made!" He does not exhibit any injured feelings, as ripe old age so often does when the younger generation tries to elbow its predecessors out of the way. England's attitude is different. She is justly proud of her great accomplishments, for they are and will continue to be her own, even though she can no longer exercise effective control over them. The fiction of Imperial unity is still useful enough for her to consent to most concessions—shall we say to all concessions?

CHAPTER IX

DOMINIONS VS. CROWN COLONIES

I. FALLING BACK ON THE COLONIAL EMPIRE

T HE British Empire is becoming too big and too vague, especially since so much of it has drifted away from central control. England seems quite ready to have her personality merged into this enlarged entity, and yet the opposite tendency is revealed by the growth of a strictly British consciousness, using "British" in the narrow sense of the word. It is not the "Little England" of the past, for we must now include Northern Ireland with Great Britain, and also the immense territories of the Crown colonies. This is an entirely different conception from the "Greater Britain" of Dilke. Though reduced in extent, the domain is still enormous, and its limits are clearly, even legally, laid down in the appendix dealing with the signature of treaties drawn up by the Imperial Conference of 1926. The area includes "Great Britain and Northern Ireland, as well as those members of the British Empire who are not separate members of the League of Nations." As the Dominions and India are separate members of the League, the above formula lays down precisely the regions over which Britain is still sovereign; but this area no longer includes the whole Empire.

Such distinctions do not appeal to the British public, who consider that they are too logical, and also that they introduce a spirit of discrimination into inter-Imperial relations. The British prefer to emphasize the unity of the Empire, leaving foreigners to analyze the subtle contrasts, the reality of which they deny. To them England and the Empire are one, and no such thing exists as an England conceived separately. They do not think of her as distinguishable from the rest, or even,—to carry the reasoning to extremes,—as opposed by the rest. Nevertheless, the old division between the Crown colonies and the self-governing Dominions is of decisive importance, especially as the latter are now not only Dominions but distinct nations.

It is no longer a question of dividing the Empire into two simple classifications, corresponding to two departments in the Colonial Office; it is much more serious than that, for already one can perceive the germs of two separate empires. In the one are grouped Canada, Australia, New Zealand, South Africa, Ireland, and Newfoundland. These are all nations of the white race, and although under the same king as England, they constitute less of a state than a community of nations. In the other empire we have England, with her Crown colonies, and up to a point, India—a political edifice corresponding more to the French idea of the State.

As the Empire increases in size it tends to split up into two or even three new empires, according to the traditional subdivisions. First we have the Dominions, which have evolved from old settlement colonies. Then come the exploitation colonies, which, although they are still developing, remain exploitation colonies. Finally, there is a third group, linked up with the second: the naval bases, coal stations, and commercial outposts scattered all over the world.

Four ministerial departments in the central Government maintain contact with the outside world: the Foreign Office deals with foreign countries, the India Office with India, the Colonial Office with the Crown colonies, and the Dominions Office with the Dominions. The creation in 1925 of a separate office for the Dominions, simply to negotiate, whereas the Colonial Office continues to administer, was symbolic of the change that has taken place.

For over half a century the autonomous colonies tolerated with growing impatience the necessity of conducting their affairs through the Colonial Office. They developed an inferiority complex, and decided that they were being looked down upon—this was true enough for many years. Today, the Secretary for the Dominions has no more authority over his correspondents than has the Foreign Secretary over his. He probably treats them with much more tact and understanding than his colleague at the Foreign Office shows towards the small powers that are so magnificently disdained by the British. The whole section of the Empire which deals through the Dominions Office should no longer be considered as "belonging" in any sense to England. This expression, which still appears quite natural to most foreigners, seems shocking, in fact perfectly absurd, to the English, and even more so to the Canadians and Australians.

Putting sentiment and prestige aside, the Mother Country, as a result of this evolution, is no longer responsible for the Dominions. As a reaction, inter-

est in the real "colonies" has revived, for, after all,
it is in this domain that British power, in its strictly
metropolitan sense, is still a reality.

2. WHAT BRITAIN CAN EXPECT FROM THE COLONIES

The reasons for this revival of interest are clear.
Individually and financially, the British never consider themselves as foreigners anywhere in the
whole Empire, but it is in the Crown Colonies that
the Englishman from England feels completely at
home, in so far as administration is concerned. The
Mother Country has the right to place her men there
as she sees fit, either as officials or colonists, and
British emigration can be directed to these lands
without the necessity of going through laborious and
even humiliating red tape in order to obtain admission. It is in this field that the long line of British
pro-consuls, who have spread out over the world
governing other races, can be continued, thus pro-
viding brilliant careers for the flower of a people
who love and understand how to rule.

Further, although local autonomy is often granted
to the colonists, their affairs are conducted according to rules drawn up by the Colonial Office. When
capital is invested, it is still under English control.

Money placed in the Dominions is largely in the form of bonds or debentures, but in the colonies, where the financial control of the Mother Country is more direct, it is chiefly in the form of shares. Venerable English corporations like the Hudson's Bay Company are an anachronism in modern Canada, developed as it is by Canadians and Americans. British initiative seems more suitably employed in the development of the African colonies.

The same reasoning, though more emphatic, can be applied to the question of raw materials. Manchester and London undoubtedly control Soudanese cotton and Malayan rubber, but Melbourne, Sydney, and Canberra reign supreme over Australian wool, and Winnipeg and Ottawa over Canadian wheat. Up to the present, London has managed to remain at the head of the Empire financially and economically, but in the Dominions it is owing to acquired position and negotiation, while in the colonies it is by authority. The creation of an economically autonomous Empire, in so far as such a thing is possible, could perhaps be more easily realized with the Crown colonies than with the Dominions. Joseph Chamberlain was, I think, the first Colonial

Secretary to appreciate and concern himself with their enormous latent resources. The widespread interest that this section of the Empire has awakened in England today, seems to date back to the Balfour of Burleigh Committee, formed during the War, and having as one of its objectives the concentrated control of the raw materials of the Empire. Today, when free trade is only a phrase, and international cartels can control the world distribution of products, England in her isolation feels more than ever the necessity for some solid territorial basis in which she would be thoroughly at home. The Empire is this basis, and this special Empire particularly so.

As the Colonial Office has been relieved of an entire section of its former activities, it is now concentrating all its efforts on the Colonial Empire. Even excluding the Dominions and India, the rest of the Empire covers a greater portion of the surface of the globe than does the French Colonial Empire, which, curiously enough, it resembles in several respects. This is undoubtedly why, in many well-informed circles in England, they are watching with entirely new attention the colonization work of the Republic. During the nineteenth century, not to mention earlier periods, France and England were inveterate rivals throughout the world, and at such times France's efforts at colonization received scant consideration from her neighbour. We French were the first to say that we did not possess the genius for colonization, and England repeated the saying after us. Latterly, however, she has perceived a striking resemblance between certain of her own problems and those which such men as Gallieni and Lyautey have had to solve, and have succeeded in solving.

This interest in French colonial affairs corresponds to a shifting of the centre of gravity of British colonial responsibility. Politically and sentimentally it is still Canada, Australia, and New Zealand that attract attention, but from the administrative and even the economic point of view, there is much more interest in Africa and Asia. In this England is drawing closer to Continental Europe, for her colonial domain is in the orbit of the Old World, while America and Oceania are so no longer. The Empire—"This sphere whose centre is everywhere and whose circumference is nowhere"—may not always have its nucleus in the British Isles, though the Crown colonies undoubtedly will continue to gravitate about the old capital. During the last generation Imperial evolution has brought this contrast strongly into the limelight.

3. TOWARDS A NEW TYPE OF EMPIRE

British colonization thus appears to divide, geographically and historically, into two separate categories. The nineteenth-century programme in the settlement colonies consisted chiefly of sending white settlers to develop the virgin soil and fill the "great open spaces." In the Crown colonies Britain is encountering complicated problems, especially during the present phase. It is no longer a question of the domestication or extermination of a semi-savage people, but rather of governing and economically utilizing great native races who often possess a high degree of civilization. Under such conditions actual settlement is of secondary importance compared with the exploitation of natural wealth by means of native man-power. In this we find in a rejuvenated form the idea of the plantation colony, which has thus regained much of the importance it had lost since the days of the Colonial Pact.

So we return to the original though now greatly

changed conception of Empire. It is less nineteenth century and Gladstonian in spirit, and more Disraelian, Dutch or even Spanish, and certainly quite different from the commonwealth type evolved during the last hundred years. Liberty and autonomy are no longer the ultimate aim—instead, we have production. Also there is an aspect of privilege, even monopoly, in favour of the Mother Country, which may lead eventually to the diminution or even the abandonment of the doctrine of the "Open Door." Except where mandate agreements or international treaties insist on equality, we must undoubtedly look for a more nationalistic spirit in the economic administration of the Empire.

This comparison with Spain may shock the Nonconformist conscience, which would not willingly admit that colonization may have as its main object the financial exploitation of a colony for the benefit of the Mother Country. Nevertheless, colonization is now the concern of Big Business, the chief aim of which is to obtain a good return on its capital. The spirit is materialistic—could it be otherwise? Certain groups have drawn up plans of campaign which, in spirit, owe little to the Liberalism of Cobden. For example, when Lord Rothermere discusses India, he seems at times to be returning to the principles of Lord North.

This does not necessarily mean that in future colonial activities will be devoid of idealism or of Liberal sentimentality. In the problems arising from the contact of different races and the clashing of various interests—as in Kenya—the British genius for colonization finds a new field of endeavour. In this respect England is now directing her efforts less to material production as in the last century, and more to the complex problems of the rights of the people. This is especially the case when there is a clash between colonists who are anxious to develop the country, and coloured races who wish to protect their rights and dignity. The great colonial administrators also have their point of view, which is simply the welfare of the general public. These men understand the coloured races, and they approach their tasks with a sense of duty which must be described as mandatorial, even when there is no question of a mandate.

This is a new phase in British history, and moreover it comes at the end of the period during which the Dominions claimed all attention. In this new and highly original atmosphere, the pursuit of money is tempered by the conscientious idealism of the governing classes, as well as by a respect for the rights of the natives, which in the days of the plantations were totally ignored. Also, in the opinion of the British Government, the full development of this part of the Empire requires the collaboration of the Dominions, who are invited to participate and whose aid is accepted with alacrity. The administration of certain territories is even confided to them. Now that Australia, New Zealand, and South Africa all have their mandates or their own Crown colonies, a zone of influence is developing around them. This policy is admitted and encouraged by the home Government, and many see in it another link between the various parts of the Empire.

Nevertheless, we must expect an eventual rivalry between the policies of the Mother Country and those of the principal Dominions. On the question of race and colour, theory and practice are very different, and the two conceptions of native treatment are by no means the same. In Africa the contrast is particularly noticeable, for on this subject the Premier of the Union of South Africa and the Governor of Kenya do not speak the same language.

The former wishes to defend himself against the blacks, while the latter is anxious to protect them. To determine the frontier between the English and the South African policy is, as may be imagined, of vital importance, as vital indeed as was the fixing of the Mason-Dixon line between the Northern and Southern States in America in the last century.

As England needs not only raw materials and food-stuffs, but also a field of action for her money, she will probably never abandon even the least of her Crown colonies. Any such request, therefore, made even in the name of peace, is not likely to succeed. Although the purchasing power of this section of the Empire is very restricted, as England sells them only some 10 per cent. of her total exports, it is a valuable market none the less, and one which she will undoubtedly try to develop.

On the other hand, are we to expect her voluntarily to hand over to the Dominions the burden of administering part of this territory? Actually she has placed the Pacific Islands in the care of Australia and New Zealand, with all the good grace of a natural gesture between members of the same family. Yet she can hardly wish to place a more extended field of action under the control of South

Africa, in view of the very different conceptions with which this Dominion is imbued. This is a delicate question, which can hardly be discussed by a foreigner. Imperial law leaves in doubt whether the Crown colonies belong to England or to the Empire, but in practice it is to England. Hence the striking contrast between the passive attitude of the Mother Country where the Dominions are concerned, and her activity and initiative in the domain over which she is still mistress.

Should the British Government concentrate on the Crown colonies, or should it on the contrary agree to disperse its activities over a broader Empire? Or should it content itself with protecting its domestic industries and home market? In each case the same difficult question arises: Dare England agree to shut herself into any self-contained system, be it ever so vast? It is evident that the British problem exceeds not merely its own national framework, but even that of "the Empire on which the sun never sets."

CHAPTER X

IS AN INTERNATIONAL BASIS
NECESSARY?

I. TRADITIONAL FACTORS

So LONG as England is organized as at present, she must depend on three essentials: first, imports, by which to supply food for her people and raw materials for her industries; secondly, exports, with which to pay, if not for all at least for two-thirds of these imports; thirdly, international exchange, with which to nourish and stimulate her general business activity. The relative importance of certain of these factors has been modified since the War, and a slightly different equilibrium has arisen spontaneously in response to the new circumstances. Yet, in spite of these changes, we are forced to conclude that England's centre of gravity remains the same as before, and that she must continue to be predominantly international. Any restriction of the freedom of exchange would risk drying up the sap on which she lives. How much more dangerous, then, to try to shut her into a closed system, be it ever so vast.

The main principles of British policy are always the same: liberty of communication and trade, international finance and control of raw materials throughout the world. One wonders whether this programme will include in the future, as it did in the past, monopoly for Britain. Perhaps she will have to struggle to maintain it, unless she is willing to share it. Whether her control be complete or limited, one fact is certain, and that is that England, constituted, as she is at present, cannot renounce this policy, and those who think otherwise are simply suffering from a severe attack of discouragement. Up to the present the authorities have never for a moment abandoned the all-important policy of the "Open Door," and any change has been in the extent of their ambition rather than in its nature. Even if England agrees to share the world with others, she herself must continue international in spirit.

The reasons which dictate this attitude are not far to seek. Freedom of communication and trade is essential for normal imports and exports without which the life of the country would cease in a few weeks. This flow of trade is as vital to England as blood is to the body, and the slightest obstruction might be fatal. England cannot compromise on this point. Today as yesterday, and as a century ago, she is ready to fight for the sake of the freedom of a strait, an isthmus, or a canal. The reserves specified by the British Government at the signing of the Kellogg Pact explicitly confirmed this policy.

"There are certain regions of the world, the welfare and integrity of which constitute a special and vital interest for our peace and safety. His Majesty's Government has been at pains to make it clear in the past that interference with these regions cannot be suffered. Their protection against attack is to the British Empire a measure of self-defence. It must be clearly understood that His Majesty's Government in Great Britain accepts the new treaty upon the distinct understanding that it does not prejudice its freedom of action in this respect."

What they had in mind was the integrity of the Suez Canal, the route to India and Australia. In the nineteenth century, England made sure of the freedom of international communications by becoming uncontested mistress of the seas, but the time may now have arrived when this all-important freedom of the seas can possibly be achieved in other ways than by being in complete control. Still, in any event, England will not tolerate, today more than yesterday, any real obstacle to communications, especially on certain trade routes.

The control of raw materials is equally necessary, for although the population of the British Isles may not require as much as they did before, owing to the falling off of business, the entrepôt trade must be kept up at all costs, and if possible England must be able to control international prices. A similar anxiety, in which the interests of industry and commerce are closely linked to those of banking, forces the City to preserve its international outlook. This it will never give up, except in the case of complete collapse, since raw materials are attracted as by a magnet towards centres where commercial transactions are financed, and international customers are likewise enticed to the sources of capital. Although diminished, the influence of the London market in foreign affairs remains an integral part of the British structure. No post-War change, no matter how important, has been able to alter this fact.

2. BRITISH POLITICAL EQUIPMENT

These essentials of power, even of existence, require political machinery. Such a machine was built up by Great Britain in the nineteenth century, and to maintain it is still an obligation on whatever party is in power.

Firstly, an overseas empire is indispensable as a territorial basis for a Mother Country which, practically speaking, has no territory of her own; also it is needed as a source of food and raw materials; as a retail market, and finally as a system of strong points the world over. Nowadays one rarely meets with the type of "Little Englander" who used to deny that England had the slightest interest in preserving her colonies.

Secondly, she must have a powerful navy to guarantee communications between the various parts of her Empire, and also to make sure that her foreign trade is not menaced. Britain is neither bellicose nor aggressive, but she must have at her disposal a repressive force to police the high seas. If any other power were to practise this policing against England, it would endanger not only her influence, but her security.

These two vital pieces in the system necessitate a third, the equipment to carry out the policy of international trade routes; for England is bound to interest herself in the great highways of the world. She must have safe passages for her mercantile marine, and such security requires judiciously chosen naval bases, and widely scattered coal and oil stations. One more point, but still part of the same scheme: she must make sure of her control not only of the ocean, but also of straits and international canals. Linked up with the trade routes is a general network of submarine cables, a system of wireless telegraphy, and, more recent creation, a series of air ports mapping out the lines of aviation. Crowning the whole, and most difficult of all to realize, she must secure a *régime* of international free trade, or at least the assurance that no tariffs or other regulations will be established to discriminate against her commerce. One cannot imagine England giving up these fundamental planks in her programme. Even if she does shut herself up within her Empire by some policy of protection, she will probably still demand liberal treatment from the rest of the world.

Finally, in this list of essential equipment, we

must place a healthy money and a credit system, radiating in all directions, and capable of serving as an instrument of international exchange. A stabilized pound on a par with the dollar is the keynote of the whole policy. That the British themselves are convinced of this is proved by the sacrifices they have made to obtain it.

3. IS A SHUT-IN SYSTEM POSSIBLE?

As a result of these unchanging conditions, England is condemned to a world-wide policy. This is not due to any plan or ambition on her part, but simply to a necessity which she feels instinctively, all the more strongly, perhaps, when she is not clearly conscious of it. Experienced pilots are essential, and therefore no other political *milieu* has ever created more great statesmen, and similarly no other nation feels so quickly the lack of leaders worthy of the name. England cannot be classed along with those well-balanced countries where the centre of gravity is low, and where government can be safely carried on by mediocrity.

During the past two years England has been sorely tempted to renounce the fundamental principles which make her great, and this must be inter-

preted as a sign of decadence. Like a weary industrialist whose factory is deteriorating, the Englishman turns to protection and preference in order to
preserve what his energy created in the past. He
is apt to envy foreigners who, having profited by
inflation, have become too strong competitors for
him. He knows he has inherited an immense empire,
though he is not sure whether or not it belongs to
him, although solid ties of sentiment and tradition
still bind it to the Motherland. The law of least resistance suggests that he should link himself more
closely to this empire, and declare it a private preserve from which poachers are excluded. Any one
who has followed English public opinion since the
War, realizes that it is dominated by the attractions of this policy of privilege and protection.
Sometimes it seems irresistible, and no one, not even
its adversaries, has the courage to oppose it openly.
Judging by the leading newspapers, by a whole
section of the ruling class, by the demand of the
industrial owners, by the trade union leaders, and
even by certain of the banks, the time is now ripe
for England to enter into a closed economic system.
The declarations along these lines, made both by the
bankers of the City and the members of the Council

of Trades Union Congress, seem to indicate un-
mistakably that the country has given up its time-
honoured policy of international freedom.

And yet when they come to the point where they
must take the first definite step, they suddenly re-
member certain elementary necessities which have
been overlooked in the heat of the discussion. A
brilliant campaign of propaganda stirred up and
excited by sentiment, is emphasizing the 42 per cent.
of exports absorbed by the Empire markets, but the
58 per cent. which the rest of the world is taking is
also making its presence strongly felt. A great fuss
may be made about the 26 per cent. of food that the
Empire supplies, but they do not forget the 74 per
cent. that comes from foreign countries. The British wish to use home-grown and Empire wheat, and
they sing the glories of Canadian and Australian
wheat-fields. Then inevitably the question arises
whether food prices will not go up, and whether if
they give up their old sources of supply, which were
also invaluable markets for British goods, the latter
may not adopt unwelcome reprisals. They boast that
they will stick to the British, or at any rate to the
English-speaking Anglo-Saxon peoples. Yet silently
there creeps in the eternal fear that foreign trade

might shrink, or that British shipping, with its deep draught, might run aground in shallow waters. In a word, one perceives that for England only an international solution is broad enough.

The typical English solution seems to be a compromise between these two tendencies, for though both exist, neither one can triumph completely over the other. They can adopt a policy of protection, from which is deleted anything incompatible with the minimum of freedom required by the British system. Perhaps we can hardly expect the complete triumph either of absolute free trade, or yet of protection with an Imperial tariff union.

At this point arises a new aspect of the situation. As the geographical equilibrium of the twentieth-century world differs from that of the nineteenth, the axis of the international trade routes do not run in exactly the same directions. Centres of attraction, which yesterday did not exist, are apparent today, and on the high seas there have appeared new powers which must be reckoned with. In the past, England's sphere of action was world wide, and she enjoyed a monopoly beyond the borders of Europe. Even though she may continue to abide by her old principles, she may in the future find herself so reduced as to be no longer international, except in certain geographic zones to which her field of action may be limited. This is simply another aspect of her shrinkage.

4. WORLD TRADE ROUTES

In the Middle Ages, when the Mediterranean was the centre of the civilized world, the British Isles lay far away beyond its orbit. Being on the outside edge of the known world, they did not act as a connecting link with any one. They were simply "Ultima Thule." But when, as a result of great discoveries, the Atlantic became the centre of the international highways going west and east, England found that circumstances had placed her at the crucial point in the world's trade routes. Whether it was a question of setting out for America, or of doubling Cape Horn or the Cape of Good Hope, no country was more favourably situated. One after another, she eliminated Spain, Portugal, Holland, and France, until in the nineteenth century she stood alone, with her maritime tentacles encircling the globe. But the Atlantic was still the centre. This accounts for the British Government's hostility to the cutting of the Suez Canal, for that meant that

the Mediterranean would again become a world
trade route, which England feared she could not
control. However, her political genius succeeded to
such a degree that this new highway became a vital
point in the communications of her Empire. In
1914, the critical year in which the Panama Canal
was opened, British supremacy on the seas was still
intact, but since then many signs of change are apparent.

From a commercial point of view the Suez route
may remain as important for England as heretofore,
but one can hardly say that its political security remains the same. The War, especially in its final
years, revealed the growing difficulty of using so
exposed a highway, owing to the new weapons of
offence that had come into existence.

Sir John Marriott, M.P., said on 4th November,
1926: "I am not certain, looking at the matter from
a distant perspective, that the instinct of those
statesmen who, from the point of view of English
diplomacy and world power, opposed the cutting of
the canal was not right. . . . If the canal had never
been made, I am not sure that our world tradition
would not be even stronger. The Mediterranean is
a very narrow sea, and the advent of the submarines

and aircraft has made it even narrower. With possible rivals on more than one shore, we might find ourselves more embarrassed than helped by the necessity of holding the canal route."

At the Liberal Summer School at Oxford in 1928, Sir Maurice Sheldon Amos, judicial adviser to the Egyptian Government from 1919 to 1925, described a similar idea. "There is a tendency in this country," he said, "to exaggerate our interests in Egypt. The circumstances in which we would want to control the Suez Canal are very rare. A great military authority told me that the Mediterranean route to the East was out of date, and if there were a war again, we should do as we did towards the end of the last War—get round by the Cape."

These are mere expressions of opinion, without official authority, but they are striking. We cannot prove it, but we have reason to believe that as far as England is concerned the Cape route is regaining the relative importance which it had lost. Suez is still a pivotal point as is shown by British policy in Egypt, but South Africa as an alternative route towards the Indian Ocean, Australasia, and the Far East, is scarcely less important. As this eastern trade is one of the mainstays of British merchant shipping, it is impossible to believe that England will abandon in the slightest degree her supremacy on either of these two routes.

On the contrary, since the War and even before that time, the trade routes which cross over the American Continent have tended to slip out of England's grasp. Two new economic nuclei, the United States and the Far East, emerged at the beginning of the twentieth century, and when they got into direct contact with each other, a new centre, rivalling Europe, was automatically developed on the Pacific. In spite of her diplomatic efforts, England has lost all control, even in the limited sense of the word, over the Panama Canal. In 1929 the British flag flew over only 27.2 per cent. of the shipping through the Panama, whereas in the Suez Canal it reached 57.1 per cent.; America's share in its own canal amounted to 45.9 per cent., but to only 2.1 per cent. in the Suez. The contrast is striking, as it emphasizes the existence of two international maritime routes, the one dominated by England and the other by the United States.

So extensive is this change in equilibrium that it even surpasses British power itself. The economic direction of the world, which ever since the Renaissance Europe conducted for her own benefit, is now contested. The coloured races are freeing themselves, and of the white races scattered all over the globe, it is the non-European section that is capturing the world's economic initiative. Therefore, as she is linked up with Europe in this matter, England finds that she is being left to one side in relation to these new constellations, whose centre is elsewhere. World supremacy, so natural to England during the last century, has become much more difficult if not actually impossible, since certain currents are no longer under her control.

Consequently, a survey of the boundaries of British aspirations becomes of the utmost importance, not merely for Great Britain herself, but also for Europe, and even for the rest of the world. We have already stressed the persistence of the international aspirations in her policy, but even while they remain international in character, they must be limited geographically. England now realizes that her influence has declined, and she agrees to give up an economic supremacy that once spread all over the world. By her titanic efforts, she succeeded in the past in overcoming any ambitious power that tried to contest her naval supremacy. The defeat of Germany, following that of Napoleon, the Dutch, and the Spanish, seemed to be the last example of this claim to complete maritime supremacy. Today, however, the United States is installed in a position which is just as menacing to England, but the latter is not in a fit condition to challenge them.

If we wish to understand the inner workings of the British policy, we must trace out the zones which England has definitely decided not to contest, and also those where she will probably maintain her right to supremacy, even against the United States. Let us try to sketch out the topography of the world as it looks today to England's rulers: First, all North America, including Canada, they regard as lost, or at any rate impossible to defend. The same is true of Central America, including the Antilles and Panama; and the north-western half of South America. This is all within the American zone. The struggle in the Far East is bitter, and England shows no signs of giving way. Elsewhere she is not abandoning anything, neither in Australasia, nor in the southern part of South America, nor, above all, in Africa and Western Asia, where direct control is definitely part of her programme.

Accordingly, the centre of gravity of British policy is not European, but is fixed almost more firmly than ever in the zones which still gravitate about Europe. We can therefore classify the great maritime routes according to the degree that they are still influenced by Great Britain. Panama is lost beyond recovery, but the Cape Horn route and the traditional link with Argentina and Uruguay will not be abandoned, neither will Suez nor the Cape of Good Hope ever be given up to any one. Although this sphere of action is still vast, it is greatly reduced in comparison with what it used to be, for England is no longer alone. Under these conditions can she maintain her former splendid economic isolation?

CHAPTER XI

INTERNATIONAL ALLIANCES

I. SPLENDID ISOLATION

ENGLAND has, in a sense, fallen between two stools, the European continent to which she does not belong, and the non-European world for which she has neither the youth nor the temperament. She is beginning to realize slowly and rather regretfully, that her splendid isolation has come to an end. Caught between a "Fordized" America and a "cartelized" Europe, she will eventually have to enter into some international economic alliance. Should she look overseas and try to fall into step with the young Anglo-Saxon countries, or should she turn back to the Old World whence came her culture? This problem is so urgent that it has become a real preoccupation to the thoughtful Englishman of today.

2. THE ANGLO-SAXON CONSTELLATION

Since the War the English have felt that they ought to break away from Europe, now torn

asunder by internal rivalries and war, and disorganized materially and morally. England has
nothing in common with such a madhouse. The old
British disdain for the foreigner has increased considerably since the Treaty of Versailles, and in any
case no Englishman ever feels that an Italian, a
German, or a Frenchman is quite his equal. Polite-
ness forbids his saying so, but he would hardly
know how to conceal his humiliation if he were included in that rabble, so he makes up his mind to
steer clear of them. It was certainly in this spirit
that the English attempted, about 1919, to re-establish the pound on a par with the dollar, leaving the
mark to be wiped out, and the franc to sicken mis-
erably. Pride insisted that the pound should not become involved in the European muddle.

When Continental affairs are not going to her
liking, her natural reaction is to fly in the opposite
direction, and seek refuge among the Anglo-Saxon
peoples. There, at any rate, she feels, she will find
people of her own race who speak her language, and
feel and reason as she does. Such sentiments do not
altogether coincide with her former condescension
towards these "colonials,"—mere "provincials,"—
nor yet are they compatible with her sarcastic attitude towards the Americans, whom she regards as

ignorant *nouveaux riches*—except of course in finance and politics. Before the War the Dominions suffered from an inferiority complex because they thought that England looked down upon them, but today England is at their feet. There are plenty of reasons to justify a recourse to Anglo-Saxon solidarity, but it must still be confessed that it relates more to customs than to culture. England's culture, which is one of the most refined in the world, obviously belongs to Europe, but because of her insularity, her customs have remained distinct, and are really more closely allied to the Empire, or even America. The same is true in the political world, where few Englishmen react in a really European way.

Many Englishmen would like to include the United States in their Anglo-Saxon family. In this they are obeying an instinct which, though well established, may not endure. Because the British Empire has spread over the entire world, English nationalism is based more on racial feelings than on attachment to the soil. Such men as Cecil Rhodes, Rosebery, Milner, and Joseph Chamberlain placed the emphasis on race, which, they contended, should be interpreted very broadly; Rhodes, especially, considered that for the unity of the Anglo-Saxon race to be complete, the Americans and even the Germans must be included with the English. Thus conceived, the Imperial circle widens beyonds the limits of the flag, and it is this interpretation of Empire which certain Dominions in the Pacific are almost unconsciously tempted to share, especially when the defence of the white race is at stake. The racial appeal, therefore, has always exerted a powerful influence on the British, and it comes to the fore whenever they feel disgusted with some Continental quarrel. England considers such bickering utterly fruitless, and declines to take any active part in it.

As we have seen, a closed economic system, based on Imperialism, no matter how wide, is insufficient. The Anglo-Saxon union to be broad enough, must include the Americans, for their collaboration, no matter how loose, is still essential. Lloyd George, Baldwin, and MacDonald, have all worked persistently to secure American co-operation and so realize this will-o'-the-wisp of post-War policy.

Many advantages are expected to accrue from such a combination. England would act as broker for the United States in the latter's economic international relations, to the mutual profit of both sides. In political negotiations she would be the interpreter, especially in all manner of European affairs, with which she has been conversant for years. The pound would be bolstered up by the dollar, and the two navies would jointly police and control the high seas. Without there being any definite political *entente,* most of this programme could be realized by tacit accord. Wall Street and the City, for example, already collaborate more than they compete. If this union were admitted—especially if it were proclaimed—it would mean much more. England would benefit from a valuable increase in prestige, for she could pride herself on being a partner on equal terms with America, the richest power in the world. Also, think of the air of moral superiority that such an *entente* could assume in dealing with tiresome people, who do not know their place! It could impose an Anglo-Saxon peace, similar to the *pax romana,* based on the irresistible police force of the two greatest navies in the world—all this, of course, being "for the greatest good of the greatest number." So, whenever they talk of an Anglo-Saxon Union, they act as if it were a duty, not a matter of self-interest.

England has not succeeded in imposing her plan on America, for over there they are still suspicious, and afraid of being made use of by "perfidious Albion." Nevertheless, the only danger in the scheme would be for England herself, for from now on the United States would certainly demand first place in any combination in which she may be included—in fact, from the American point of view, this goes without saying. Therefore, in any Anglo-American *entente,* the British Government runs the risk of being reduced to the rank of a "brilliant second"; moreover, if any Anglo-Saxon constellation evolves, it is quite possible that it may not gravitate around Old England.

Is England even certain of remaining the centre of her own Empire? Yes, so far as sentiment is concerned, for the whole race is faithful to the memory of its origin, and looks with reverence upon the old country. Yet the Dominions today insist so strongly on preserving their independence in the managing of their own affairs, and on keeping themselves free to make their own alliances, even with foreign countries, that the conception of an Empire, solidly grouped around the British metropolis, has less hope of realization than before. Many of the English

Imperialists, indeed, are the first to discard the idea. They will even discuss whether the capital might not just as well be in Ottawa as in London, and whether the value of the Imperial conception would thereby be diminished. They feel that they will always be the brains of this great body politic, but they no longer insist that they must be the executive as well.

We must not overlook the possible danger which any kind of centrifugal attractions may hold for the Empire, constituted as it is at present. Certain of the Dominions tend to gravitate more and more around the United States, where they find the same standard of living as they enjoy, the same needs, the same economic youthfulness, the same conception of the white race, and the same attitude towards the coloured races. There is nothing political in this, for their loyalty is unquestionable, and they have, if anything, an antipathy for the United States. It is simply one of those appeals which exceeds political limits. Eventually this new centre of gravity may cause a whole section of the British constellation to rotate in a different orbit—how inevitably one thinks of the movement of celestial bodies!

This idea is seldom mentioned, in either the British or the colonial press, for a natural delicacy prevents them from discussing it. One politician, however, Sir Auckland Geddes, was not afraid to express it. In a speech delivered in Toronto, in November 1924, he said: "The British Dominions which look out upon the Pacific feel that in Washington there is an instinctive understanding of their difficulties which, when they come to London, they have to explain laboriously to Downing Street. When the Dominions look to the Mother Country and find no satisfactory understanding, they naturally turn to Washington; and Washington, not being devoid of eyes, will look back to them." As this speech aroused considerable protest, it must not be accepted to the letter, but in spirit it is correct, and should not be neglected.

Hence, the centre of gravity of the British Empire is tending to move away from England, and the more Imperialism becomes a reality, the more this is so. At the same time, Britain sees with growing clearness that her supremacy is again contested, and now by the very power with whom she is ready to associate herself. Since the United States became a world force, a logical and irresistible evolution has tended to shape its international policy on the same lines as England's. Both are pursuing the same three-cornered programme: control of raw materials, international finance, and maritime communications. In consequence, they both feel the need of the same kind of political equipment.

On the eve of the Washington Conference in 1921 *The Times* was the first to remark that America was finding that she required an international policy in the full sense of the term. "From being simply a commercial nation," *The Times* noted, "she has passed at one bound to a directing position among the financial powers. She now realizes to what extent this fact must react on her relations with the outside world. The opportunity is there, but the United States is unprepared, not having the political equipment necessary to take advantage of it. For the first time she realizes the full significance of world communications, *i.e.* mercantile marine, safe commercial routes, petrol and coaling stations, and cables, and of the part these things play in relation to her own national interests."

This medley of interests and aspirations results in a maritime policy which endangers Britain's supremacy. England can no longer institute a blockade except in agreement and active collaboration with America. Meanwhile the American Navy in turn is striving to control communications, or at any rate certain international routes. England is seeking an ally, but she may find a rival.

3. ENGLAND AND THE UNITED STATES

At this point the psychology of Anglo-American relations becomes really difficult to understand, and a foreigner is not sure of his ground. Rivalry between England and the United States undoubtedly exists, but their co-operation is equally certain. The French are ready to believe that they hate each other and will end up with a fight. Yet there is no denying the fact that they become reconciled whenever a third party is present, and no one can possibly be allied with either of them against the other, for they are sure to unite behind one's back. Questions of race, family, tradition, and self-interest are all extraordinarily mixed up in their relationship.

In order to preserve her supremacy on the seas, England has, in little over a century, waged two great wars, one against the France of Napoleon, and the other against Germany under William II. In each case she was all but exhausted. Today, in a mere decade, without a war, without a struggle, without seeming to care, this same England—is she the same?—has renounced her supremacy, at least in principle, at the request of the United States. We are forced to regard this renunciation as a loss of prestige. The English would have you believe that it is simply common sense, and that it had to be done. If they feel humiliated they certainly do not show it. Furthermore, Balfour and MacDonald, the two men who in 1921 and 1929 negotiated the agreements which led to the present solution, both returned home from Washington in triumph. How do the British really feel about it in their innermost hearts?

Since the beginning of the century the British Government seems to have made up its mind never to oppose the United States. It invariably gives way, as if it had decided always to do so. This recalls the line of Corneille: *"Ah, ne me brouillez pas avec la République!"*

England finds that she is faced with a growing force against which frontal resistance counts but little. She also knows that in the case of conflict between the two nations, it would be difficult for Canada to take the side of the Mother Country. At best, there might be civil war in the Dominion, which would mean that both the war and the Dominion would be lost in the end. As those in authority are aware of this, they would not lightly risk rupture, indeed they would do everything to avoid it. Little by little this reasoning is being applied not only to Canada, but to all British possessions lying within the American zone. In practice everything remains the same as long as the United States says nothing, but what is the good of sovereignty if you forbid yourself to exercise it? In the whole zone covered by the Monroe Doctrine, the fiction of sovereignty persists, although it is no longer complete—simply, it must not be mentioned. The vase is cracked. Do not touch it.

England feels that she is confronted by a sort of elemental force, and has therefore put to one side all thought of competition in armaments. In 1921 naval equality was still looked upon as a concession on her part, but now it is the turn of the United States to think that they are being generous in not asking for more than equality. Why do they not do so? After all, equality to them represents actual supremacy in their own zone, because their forces are concentrated, whereas the British forces are scattered. As far as Europe is concerned, the British

Government is determined to resist, and still maintains its old two-power standard. As regards the United States, however, it has given way, thus reversing its century-old policy.

In what spirit have the British people received this new attitude, so little in keeping with their traditional pride? It has not affected the masses, and in the upper classes an important section, probably the most important, has accepted the *fait accompli* without grumbling. We would be perhaps right in saying that in this matter England tolerates from the United States what she would never tolerate from any other power. "Needs must . . ." the English seem to say. "The Americans are not absolute strangers. We both have the same origin, the same civilization, and the same language—almost! After all, we made them! We know—or at least we prefer to believe—that when they build a fleet equal to ours they have no aggressive intentions against us. With Napoleon or William II it was entirely different. In the future the British and American fleets will work together to police the seas and maintain the peace of the world, and it will be an Anglo-Saxon peace. There is surely neither objection nor humiliation in that?" If they were dealing with a foreign power such reasoning would be defeatist.

Perhaps they simply consider that the Empire must eventually dissolve into a greater Anglo-Saxon *ensemble*. "We must co-operate with America," the Imperialists say, "for with us it is a question of sentiment as well as necessity. As our economic structure is not European, it involves working in harmony with the Dominions, and they would not accept a clash with the American point of view. Therefore our hands are tied. Who knows, but that in the last analysis the United States may be compelled to build a fleet much stronger than ours, in order to guarantee the freedom of the seas and the communications between the English-speaking peoples of the world. If the Empire is destined to disappear, it could be replaced, to a certain extent, by a union of English-speaking peoples, which would bring the Anglo-Saxon race still more powerfully together."

This attitude is difficult for the French to understand, but amongst the English and even more among the colonials, it represents a rooted conviction. The union of the Anglo-Saxon powers has no political basis owing to the fundamental rivalry between England and the United States, yet from the ethnical and religious points of view certain Anglo-Saxon and American reactions are similar. The American of the Middle West, moulded by the Ku-Klux-Klan, and the Orangemen of Belfast, will often react in the same way, but both will always be incomprehensible to the French. This reaction to the United States partially explains Britain's lassitude in not striving to retain by force her political control of the world. She is beginning to feel old. She naturally makes way for youth, especially since the youth is a member of her own family.

All this is being said in England, it is pondered over, and fully appreciated. The bitterness, nevertheless, goes deep. Though their political watchword ought to be friendship, the English can hardly contain their antipathy for their American cousins. They rail against their accent, their manners, and their lack of culture; for the first time they show an inferiority complex towards these all-powerful *nouveaux riches*. In their humiliation they hope that they have made no decisive concessions. "Even if the Americans do build this fleet," they say, "will they know how to use it? Will they ever be able to man it? Seamanship requires long training, and cannot be improvised." They consider that the United

States, being essentially a continental country, is ill-prepared for a seafaring life. Also, it is scarcely better equipped for the complications of international commerce and politics. They comfort themselves with the thought that for years to come, America will need them to act as intermediary.

Let us suppose that the two nations do come to an accord, though only a tacit one. One can foresee that their combined fleets might dominate the world, at any rate outside of Europe, for the benefit of the two Anglo-Saxon powers. Though England is apparently ready to follow in the wake, she intends to dictate the course to be followed. For example, she has given up the form of blockade which would not be acceptable to the Washington Government, but she thinks that when the time comes she will be able to persuade America that such a blockade is in the interests of them both, or still better, that it is their obvious duty.

Under our very eyes a *régime* of maritime domination is giving way almost imperceptibly to a new *régime,* in which the freedom of the seas will be under Anglo-Saxon rather than purely English control. If this new *régime* is to function, there must never be a definite clash with the United States.

This is possible only so long as American ambition does not venture beyond the zone which England is resigned to let her dominate. By paying this price, the Empire can exist indefinitely in its present form, and British commerce can prosper. More than one decision in British policy has already been altered to conform with the American point of view. Given the choice of Europe in decline and America full of life, England feels that her best course is to turn towards vitality. But perhaps all Englishmen do not reason in this way.

4. ENGLAND AND THE CONTINENT

Once, when talking to a Canadian, I referred to England as part of Europe, and I was quite surprised when he exclaimed, "But England is not in Europe!" This attitude is fairly general, not only in Canada and the Dominions, but also in the United States, and even in England herself. In the minds of the Anglo-Saxons the "Europeanness" of Great Britain is not complete. Here is the Continent, and the British Isles lie over there on the edge, but they are not the same thing. This view-point must be borne in mind when discussing England's relations with Europe. The English always seem to be onlookers who wish to keep themselves free to enter other combinations. The attractions of the non-European world are really too strong for this people, who are already spread out all over the globe, with kinships and interests in every corner. I know many Englishmen who go twice as often to the Cape or to New York as they do to Paris. In France they are out of their element, foreigners and far from home. We might liken England to a ship which, though anchored in European waters, is always ready to sail away.

This is all true, but the opposite is equally true. So much so that the real situation has the appearance of being a compromise between two contrary forces, or may even be regarded as a debate between two Englishmen, one of whom feels he is European and the other does not. England cannot cut herself entirely adrift from the Continent which lies so close to her, any more than Europe can consider herself complete without those two little islands which lie at her gates. Neither politically, economically, nor intellectually, can one long admit the thesis of a non-European England, out of touch with the old world.

From a political point of view England's geographic proximity to the Continent absolutely forbids her disinteresting herself in its affairs. The Napoleonic Wars, the Great War of 1914, and since then the Locarno Pact, all go to prove this. Economically it is the same. In 1929, 31.3 per cent. of her exports went to Europe, and this proportion is regaining the ground lost since 1913, when it was 34.6 per cent. Also it was from the Continent that England purchased, in 1929, 37.4 per cent. of her imports, in other words, more than from any other part of the world. As for re-exports, Europe absorbs 68.6 per cent. in comparison with 56 per cent. in 1913. As North America breaks away from the British entrepôt trade, its commerce is being replaced by goods destined for Europe; in fact, America now takes only 19.8 per cent. of Britain's re-exports as against 32.3 per cent. before the War. Europe is therefore an irreplaceable market, and England realizes that her prosperity rises and falls in sympathy with that of the old world. It is sheer folly to think that she can disentangle herself from Europe.

Finally, the English people are deeply Europeanized in culture. The England of Shakespeare, whose intellectual outlook has so strongly influenced the whole British character, will not, in the long run, accommodate itself to any system dominated by non-European elements. England will not be able to recognize herself in a greater Anglo-Saxon Empire, where values will have surreptitiously become American rather than English. As long as colonial life remained under British control, the homeland was enriched by the Anglo-colonial civilization, which still belonged to her. If outside influences should weaken the Mother Country so that she is unable to compete within the Empire against a new non-British civilization, is it to be hoped that her culture can be preserved intact, even within her own borders? Many Englishmen now realize that this protection of English culture is bound up with the protection of European culture.

In the list of European and non-European influences, the arguments are about equal on both sides. This explains why, for the past two or three generations, and especially since the War, British statesmen have been hesitating at the cross-roads. Some, believing that their country cannot disinterest itself from Continental affairs, are not afraid to consider themselves as Europeans. Others feel that Europe is dangerous ground, and full of ambushes, foreign in every sense of the word. "Better leave it alone: *suave mari magno,*" they say prudently.

This very hesitation is the clue to the British attitude. England must deal with non-European factors which Europe does not understand. On the Continent she is chiefly interested in maintaining peace, for in the event of a war she fears that sooner or later she would be drawn in. She has no aspirations beyond the desire for a state of peace in which no one dominates. Such was her attitude when she participated in Locarno, for in this respect she admitted that she was European and interested in what transpires in a field of action so adjacent to her own. The Dominions, who scrutinize her policy closely, admit that for her this attitude is reasonable. They approve of her being European in what concerns her alone, but they refuse to associate themselves with her in these matters, and especially to undertake the slightest obligation which might involve them in war. In case of necessity the non-European parts of the Empire would adopt a passive belligerency, but nothing further. If England exceeds these limits, and lets herself be drawn into a series of alliances, or become too closely linked up with the Continent, she may lose the help of the Empire, or even imperil its very existence. What a delicate situation!

Unless the Continent forces her to choose between Europe on the one hand and the United States on the other—in these problems the Dominions and the United States may be considered as one—England possibly can carry on indefinitely in contact with both sides. If she is forced to decide, she will side against Europe—today, at any rate—in favour of the English-speaking countries of the world. The Imperialists thus express a deep national instinct when they insist that England must not proclaim herself a European instead of a world power. It is in this spirit that British policy has, for some years now, been seriously limited in two respects. England cannot do anything which will displease the Dominions—though, of course, she can shelter behind them to refuse proposals which she herself does not care to entertain—nor can she risk a quarrel with the United States. It is with exactly the same reserves that British industry maintains contact with the European cartels, and in certain cases adheres to them.

There is no reason to believe that this centrifugal attraction away from Europe will finally carry the day. Europe, and France especially, has its own views on the matter. In France we believe that England is an essential piece in the European mechanism, a vital link as it were between Europe and the other continents. It is chiefly through England that Europe is in contact with different parts of the world. Also that a large proportion of the world's raw materials are drawn into the British entrepôt market, to be later distributed on the Continent. Lastly, it is through her that the Dominions continue to gravitate about the old birthplace of civilization.

England as the international broker, or foreign agent for the old world, could not safely be dispensed with. We appreciate the advantage of having at our doors the London warehouse, where we can buy and sell the products of the whole world with a profusion of choice. We also realize the profits that international trade has reaped during the past century from the economic liberty that prevails wherever the English establish themselves. Under such conditions we cannot be indifferent to the attitude that England adopts towards her Empire, even towards her place in that Empire. It is a serious concern to us whether the centre of gravity of the system is to be in London or a thousand miles away, or even on some roving ship, where, according to an Imperialistic poet, the future government of the Anglo-Saxon races should be installed. It is even more important to us for the center of the English-speaking world to remain within the Empire, where European influence, though reduced, can still be felt. Otherwise it might slip altogether out of our orbit into some distant society, which, though friendly, is impervious to European influence, and on which our influence is nil. If England were to renounce her European position and become merely a partner in the great Anglo-Saxon community of nations, we could not but feel that something in ourselves had been struck down. Perhaps certain Englishmen think so too.

5. CONTRADICTORY ATTRACTIONS

England's entire structure has been shaken by the War, and even more so by the evolution that has taken place all over the world during the last half century. We have now reviewed the various solutions that present themselves to England in her efforts to re-establish her equilibrium, but whatever her choice may be, certain inconveniences must be

coped with. If she shuts herself in behind a tariff
she weakens herself and risks drying up the springs
that feed her commercial and financial activities.

If, on the other hand, she tries to preserve her
world-wide influence and stand alone as before,
without international alliances, she may not now
be strong enough. Can she set up a system independent of America and Europe, now that both are
organizing themselves industrially, each in its own
way?

Or if, relying on the aid of the Dominions, she
agrees to enclose herself within the broad framework of her Empire, she is nevertheless renouncing that liberty of outlook which hitherto knew no
bounds. Far-off influences might be forced upon her,
and be insinuated into her policy. If she hitches her
waggon to the American star, it is much the same,
for in each case she may possibly lose control.

If, finally, she unites herself with Europe she risks
losing the help of her Dominions, who are determined not to compromise their youth with the declining age of the Continent, whose best days may
be over. In this case, the British system might turn
towards the Crown colonies, which still gravitate
about Europe. Britain would then become more

strictly English and European in policy and culture. What is much more likely is that England will not choose at all. Faithful to her tradition and her genius, she will hover between the two groups, without giving herself completely either to one or to the other. A European England is a dream, and a closed Empire a Utopia. Vitality and flexibility have always been the strongest traits of the British nation. As M. Renier has said, so long as her Empire communications are assured and her money is healthy, she can adapt herself to any international system whatsoever. When England changes, we say she is dying, and it is never true. The Empire, and the spirit of England on which it thrives, have unlimited powers of adaptation and life.

INDEX